Better Homes and Gardens®

Brown Bagger's Cook Book

© Copyright 1985 by Meredith Corporation, Des Moines, Iowa.
All Rights Reserved. Printed in the United States of America.
First Edition. Second Printing, 1985.
Library of Congress Catalog Card Number: 84-61311
ISBN: 0-696-01472-6 (hard cover)
ISBN: 0-696-01470-X (trade paperback)

BETTER HOMES AND GARDENS® BOOKS

Editor: Gerald M. Knox
Art Director: Ernest Shelton
Managing Editor: David A. Kirchner

Food and Nutrition Editor: Nancy Byal
Department Head—Cook Books: Sharyl Heiken
Associate Department Heads: Sandra Granseth,
    Rosemary C. Hutchinson, Elizabeth Woolever
Senior Food Editors: Julia Malloy, Marcia Stanley,
    Joyce Trollope
Associate Food Editors: Barbara Atkins, Molly Culbertson,
    Linda Foley, Linda Henry, Lynn Hoppe, Jill Johnson,
    Mary Jo Plutt, Maureen Powers
Recipe Development Editor: Marion Viall
Test Kitchen Director: Sharon Stilwell
Test Kitchen Photo Studio Director: Janet Pittman
Test Kitchen Home Economists: Jean Brekke, Kay Cargill,
    Marilyn Cornelius, Maryellyn Krantz, Lynelle Munn,
    Dianna Nolin, Marge Steenson, Cynthia Volcko

Associate Art Directors: Linda Ford Vermie,
    Neoma Alt West, Randall Yontz
Copy and Production Editors: Marsha Jahns,
    Mary Helen Schiltz, Carl Voss, David A. Walsh
Assistant Art Directors: Harijs Priekulis, Tom Wegner
Senior Graphic Designers: Alisann Dixon,
    Lynda Haupert, Lyne Neymeyer
Graphic Designers: Mike Burns, Mike Eagleton,
    Deb Miner, Stan Sams, Darla Whipple-Frain

Vice President, Editorial Director: Doris Eby
Executive Director, Editorial Services: Duane L. Gregg

Senior Vice President, General Manager: Fred Stines
Director of Publishing: Robert B. Nelson
Vice President, Retail Marketing: Jamie Martin
Vice President, Direct Marketing: Arthur Heydendael

BROWN BAGGER'S COOK BOOK

Editor: Molly Culbertson
Copy and Production Editor: David A. Walsh
Graphic Designer: Harijs Priekulis
Contributing Photographers: Mike Dieter;
    M. Jensen Photography, Inc.
Food Stylists: Janet Pittman, Maria Rolandelli
Contributing Illustrator: Thomas Rosborough

Our seal assures you that every recipe in *Brown Bagger's
Cook Book* has been tested in the Better Homes and Gardens®
Test Kitchen. This means that each recipe is practical
and reliable, and meets our high standards of taste appeal.

On the cover: The possibilities for creative brown-
bag sandwiches are limitless, as you can see by
this sandwich fantasy. See pages 20 and 21 for tips on
putting together your own sandwich creation.

Contents

Sandwiches and More

Sandwiches any way you like them—we've got them! We've layered fillings between delicious purchased and home-baked breads, and tucked them inside baked sandwiches to make these lunch-box stuffers worth toting! And that's just the beginning. How about a hearty stew, a crisp, light salad, or an elegant pâté for your take-along lunch? With every recipe, you'll find the packing and carrying tips to ensure easy, great-tasting brown-bag meals.

Devilicious Ham Sandwiches
(see recipe, page 7)

Shrimp Cocktail Pockets
(see recipe, page 16)

Cheesy Egg Sandwiches
(see recipe, page 7)

Crab-Filled Croissants
(see recipe, page 16)

**Double Cheese-
Hamwiches**
(see recipe, page 19)

**Salmon-Stuffed French
Rolls** (see recipe, page 12)

**Mediterranean
Sandwiches**
(see recipe, page 19)

Making It Safe, Keeping It Fresh

It's easy to keep your take-along lunch safe and fresh tasting throughout the longest morning. Just follow our simple tips:
- Be sure anything that touches the food is very clean.
- Seal foods in clean airtight containers or clear plastic storage bags.
- Chill cold foods overnight. Then, in the morning, pack them in prechilled insulated vacuum containers (see tip, page 46) or in insulated lunch boxes with frozen ice packs.
- Pack hot foods *hot* in preheated insulated vacuum containers (see tip, page 46).
- Use *new* lunch bags or *clean* lunch boxes.
- Keep your lunch in a *cool* dry place all morning.

Fruited Cheese Pockets

½ cup cream-style cottage cheese
½ cup shredded Monterey Jack cheese (2 ounces)
1 8¾-ounce can fruit cocktail, drained
2 tablespoons sliced almonds
1 to 2 tablespoons milk (optional)

- In a small bowl stir together the cottage cheese, shredded Monterey Jack cheese, fruit cocktail, and sliced almonds. Add enough of the milk to moisten, if necessary; mix well. Divide the mixture between 2 small airtight containers. Store up to 1 week in the refrigerator. Makes enough filling for 2 sandwiches.

Lettuce leaves
Large pita bread round, split crosswise

- For *each* serving, in the morning pack *1* lettuce leaf and *1* pita half in separate small clear plastic bags. Carry with *1* container of the *chilled* mixture in an insulated lunch box with an ice pack.

At lunchtime, line the pita pocket with lettuce. Spoon in the fruit-and-cheese mixture, as shown at right.

Remember to pack a spoon with your lunch. Then, at serving time, spoon the fruit-and-cheese mixture into the lettuce-lined pita pocket.

Cheesy Egg Sandwiches

Pictured on page 4.

½ cup mayonnaise *or* salad dressing ¼ teaspoon dry mustard ⅛ teaspoon garlic salt	● In a small bowl stir together the mayonnaise or salad dressing, dry mustard, and garlic salt.
3 hard-cooked eggs, chopped 1 cup shredded cheddar cheese (4 ounces) ¼ cup finely chopped celery 3 tablespoons sunflower nuts 2 tablespoons sliced green onion	● Stir in the chopped hard-cooked eggs, shredded cheddar cheese, chopped celery, sunflower nuts, and sliced green onion. Cover and store up to 1 week in the refrigerator. Makes enough spread for 4 sandwiches.
Sandwich bread Lettuce leaves (optional) Tomato slices	● For *each* serving, in the morning spread ½ *cup chilled* filling onto *1 slice* of bread. Add *1* lettuce leaf, if desired (for crisper lettuce, pack in a separate plastic bag). Top with *another slice* of bread. Pack the sandwich in a small clear plastic bag. Pack *2* or *3 slices* of tomato in a separate small clear plastic bag. Carry all in an insulated lunch box with a frozen ice pack. At mealtime, add the tomato slices to the sandwich.

Even when you make your sandwich hours before lunch, it won't get soggy with this flavorful filling of eggs, cheese, and crunchy sunflower nuts. Because this filling is drier than many others, you can add lettuce when you make the sandwich instead of packing it separately.

Devilicious Ham Sandwiches

Pictured on page 4.

1 4½-ounce can deviled ham 1 3-ounce package cream cheese, softened 2 tablespoons chopped green pepper 2 tablespoons chopped pimiento Dash hot pepper sauce 6 slices sandwich bread *or* 3 bagels, split	● In a small bowl stir together the deviled ham and softened cream cheese. Add the chopped green pepper, chopped pimiento, and hot pepper sauce. Stir till well mixed. Spread onto *3 slices* of sandwich bread or *3* bagel halves. Top with remaining bread or bagel halves. Pack each sandwich in a freezer bag. Store up to 1 month in the freezer. Makes 3 sandwiches.
Lettuce leaves	● For *each* serving, in the morning pack *1* or *2* lettuce leaves in a small clear plastic bag. Carry with *1 frozen* sandwich in a brown bag with a frozen ice pack. The sandwich will thaw in 4 to 6 hours. At mealtime, add the lettuce to the ham sandwich.

Give your sandwich a flavor and protein boost by adding a slice or two of your favorite cheese. Wrap the cheese in a separate small clear plastic bag and pack it in your brown bag. At lunchtime, add the cheese to your sandwich.

Bean Burritos

¼ cup sliced green onion
1 small clove garlic, minced
1 tablespoon cooking oil
½ of a 15-ounce can refried beans (about 1 cup)
1 tablespoon chopped canned green chili peppers

● In a skillet cook the sliced green onion and minced garlic in hot cooking oil till onion is tender but not brown. Add the refried beans and chopped green chili peppers; cook and stir till the mixture is heated through.

For a Mexican lunchtime fiesta that will make you the envy of other brown baggers, pack these easy burritos. Add an apple and a small insulated vacuum bottle filled with your favorite soup to round out the meal.

2 10-inch flour tortillas
½ cup shredded cheddar cheese (2 ounces)
1 small tomato, seeded and chopped
2 tablespoons sliced green onion

● Spoon about *½ cup* bean mixture onto *each* tortilla near one edge. Top with *¼ cup* cheddar cheese, *half* of the tomato, and *half* of the sliced green onion. Fold the edge nearest the filling up and over filling, just till mixture is covered. Fold in two sides envelope style, then roll up. Pack each burrito in a small clear plastic bag. Store up to 3 days in the refrigerator. Makes 2 burritos.

Try the burritos hot, too. To reheat *one* burrito, place on a *white* paper plate. Micro-cook, uncovered, on HIGH for 35 to 40 seconds. Micro-cook *two* burritos, uncovered, on HIGH for 1 minute to 1 minute and 15 seconds.

● For *each* serving, in the morning pack *1* or *2* burritos in a brown bag.

Pork-Curry Pockets

½ cup mayonnaise *or* salad dressing
¼ teaspoon curry powder
1 cup finely chopped cooked pork
¼ cup shredded carrot
¼ cup coconut
2 tablespoons finely chopped green pepper

● In a small bowl stir together the mayonnaise or salad dressing and curry powder. Stir in the finely chopped pork, shredded carrot, coconut, and finely chopped green pepper. Mix well. Divide mixture among 3 small airtight containers. Store mixture up to 1 week in the refrigerator. Makes enough filling for 3 sandwiches.

With just a little leftover pork roast, you can make these tropical sandwich pockets. To complement the curry flavor, take along something cool and refreshing, such as a fresh peach or pineapple chunks packed in a small airtight container.

Large pita bread rounds, halved, *or* sandwich bread

● For *each* serving, in the morning pack *2* pita halves or *2 slices* of sandwich bread in a small clear plastic bag. Carry with *1 container* of the *chilled* pork mixture in an insulated lunch box with a frozen ice pack.
  At mealtime, spoon the pork mixture into pita halves, or assemble a sandwich with the bread.

Chicken Salad Croissants

1 8-ounce can crushed pineapple (juice pack)
1 teaspoon cornstarch
¼ teaspoon ground ginger
¼ teaspoon salt
⅓ cup mayonnaise *or* salad dressing

● For dressing, in a small saucepan combine the *undrained* pineapple, cornstarch, ginger, and salt. Cook and stir over medium heat till thickened and bubbly. Cook and stir 2 minutes more. Cool. Add the mayonnaise or salad dressing. Stir to mix well.

1 cup chopped cooked chicken
¼ cup chopped green pepper
¼ cup sliced almonds, toasted

● In a small bowl combine the chicken, green pepper, and almonds. Add the pineapple dressing; stir to mix well. Divide between 2 small airtight containers. Store mixture up to 1 week in the refrigerator. Makes enough filling for 2 sandwiches.

Whole wheat *or* white croissants, split
Bibb lettuce *or* lettuce leaves

● For *each* serving, in the morning pack *1* whole wheat or white croissant and a *small amount* of Bibb lettuce or *1* lettuce leaf in separate small clear plastic bags. Carry with *1 container* of the *chilled* chicken mixture in an insulated lunch box with a frozen ice pack.

At lunchtime, assemble the croissant, the lettuce, and the chicken salad mixture into a sandwich.

The tropical pineapple and ginger flavors in this filling go well with a wide selection of breads, from bakery croissants to homemade whole wheat slices. We recommend Oatmeal-Raisin Braid (see recipe, page 26), Whole Wheat-Pecan Loaf (see recipe, page 23), or Granana Batter Bread (see recipe, page 25).

Turkey-Relish Supreme

1 5-ounce can chunk-style turkey *or* chicken, drained and chopped
¼ cup cranberry-orange relish
¼ cup shredded Swiss *or* cheddar cheese (1 ounce)
3 tablespoons mayonnaise *or* salad dressing
2 tablespoons finely chopped celery
2 tablespoons chopped pecans

● In a bowl combine the chopped chunk-style turkey or chicken, cranberry-orange relish, shredded Swiss or cheddar cheese, mayonnaise or salad dressing, finely chopped celery, and chopped pecans. Stir to mix well.

Divide between 2 small airtight containers. Store the mixture up to 1 week in the refrigerator. Makes enough filling for 2 sandwiches.

Sandwich bread
Lettuce leaves

● For *each* serving, in the morning pack *2 slices* of bread and *1* lettuce leaf in separate small clear plastic bags. Carry with *1 container* of the *chilled* turkey mixture in an insulated lunch box with a frozen ice pack.

At lunchtime, assemble the bread, lettuce leaf, and the turkey-relish mixture into a sandwich.

All insulated containers are not alike. Thick mixtures like this filling stay colder longer in an insulated lunch box with a frozen ice pack. Use insulated vacuum bottles when you want to keep saucier mixtures such as soups hot or cold.

Plan an elegant lunch with a friend, and take Chicken Salad Croissants. Just put *all* of the chicken mixture into *one* airtight container before chilling. Take *two* croissants and extra lettuce. For dessert, include in-season fresh fruit. Add bright paper napkins, and you're ready for lunchtime entertaining. (Don't forget a spoon for assembling the sandwiches.)

Salmon-Stuffed French Rolls

Pictured on page 5.

½	cup chopped broccoli *or* cauliflower flowerets	● In a bowl toss together the chopped broccoli or cauliflower flowerets, shredded carrot, and chopped cucumber.
¼	cup shredded carrot	
¼	cup chopped cucumber	

⅓	cup mayonnaise *or* salad dressing	● Stir in the mayonnaise or salad dressing, dillweed, and pepper. Fold in the flaked salmon. Divide among 3 small airtight containers. Store mixture up to 1 week in the refrigerator. Makes enough filling for 3 sandwiches.
½	teaspoon dried dillweed	
⅛	teaspoon pepper	
1	7¾-ounce can salmon, drained, slightly flaked, and skin and bones removed	

| | French-style rolls, split, *or* sandwich bread Green pepper rings | ● For *each* serving, in the morning pack 1 roll or *2 slices* of bread and *2 or 3* green pepper rings in separate small clear plastic bags. Carry roll or bread and green pepper with *1 container* of the *chilled* salmon mixture in an insulated lunch box with a frozen ice pack. At lunchtime, assemble roll or bread, salmon mixture, and green pepper rings into a sandwich. |

Vary the flavor of this or just about any of our other terrific sandwich fillings by layering different vegetables in your sandwich. Try sliced radishes, tomato slices, bean sprouts, cucumber slices, shredded carrot, or thinly sliced green onion in place of (or in addition to) the green pepper rings. Just pack the vegetables in a small clear plastic bag, and add them to your sandwich at lunchtime.

Hot Dog Pockets

½	cup baked beans	● In a small bowl stir together the baked beans, frankfurter slices, shredded American cheese, French salad dressing, and finely chopped onion. Pack in an airtight container. Store mixture up to 1 week in the refrigerator. Makes enough filling for 1 sandwich.
1	frankfurter, sliced crosswise	
¼	cup shredded American cheese (1 ounce)	
2	tablespoons sweet French salad dressing	
1	tablespoon finely chopped onion	

| 1 | large pita bread round, split crosswise | ● For 1 serving, in the morning pack the pita halves and lettuce in separate small clear plastic bags. Carry with the *chilled* baked bean mixture in an insulated lunch box with a frozen ice pack. At serving time, line each pita pocket with a lettuce leaf. Spoon *half* of the baked bean filling into *each* pocket. |
| 2 | lettuce leaves | |

Please kids of all ages with this hearty hot dog and bean combo. Pita bread "pockets" neatly hold the saucy filling. (*Little* kids may want just one pocket.)

Peanut Butter-Sunshine Sandwiches

Pictured on page 14.

¾ cup chunk-style peanut butter ¼ cup orange juice ⅓ cup chopped raisins	● In a small bowl combine the peanut butter and the orange juice. Stir till well mixed. Stir in the raisins. Pack in an airtight container. Store up to 1 month in the refrigerator. Makes enough spread for 3 sandwiches.
Sandwich bread	● For *each* serving, in the morning spread about ⅓ *cup* of peanut butter mixture onto *1 slice* of bread. Top with *another slice.* Pack in a small clear plastic bag. Carry in a brown bag.

For quick packing later, make three sandwiches at once. Wrap them in freezer bags and store up to one month in the freezer.

Cheesy BLTs

½ cup cream-style cottage cheese, drained 1 3-ounce package cream cheese with chives, softened ¼ cup shredded American cheese (1 ounce) Several dashes bottled hot pepper sauce 6 slices bacon, crisp-cooked, drained, and crumbled 1 medium tomato, seeded and chopped	● Press drained cottage cheese through a sieve into a medium bowl, as shown at right. Add the softened cream cheese, the American cheese, and hot pepper sauce. Stir till well mixed. Stir in the bacon and tomato. Pack in an airtight container. Store up to 1 week in the refrigerator. Makes enough spread for 3 or 4 sandwiches.
Sandwich bread Lettuce leaves	● For *each* serving, in the morning spread about ⅓ to ½ *cup* of the *chilled* mixture onto *1 slice* of sandwich bread; top with *another slice* of bread. Pack in a small clear plastic bag. Pack lettuce leaves in a separate plastic bag. Carry sandwich and lettuce in an insulated lunch box with a frozen ice pack.

Use the back of a large spoon to gently press the drained cottage cheese through a sieve.

Peanut Butter-Pineapple Deluxe

⅔ cup chunk-style peanut
    butter
½ of a 3-ounce package
    cream cheese, softened
½ cup drained crushed
    pineapple
¼ cup shredded carrot
8 slices sandwich bread

● In a small bowl stir together the peanut butter and softened cream cheese. Stir in the crushed pineapple and shredded carrot.

Spread mixture on *4 slices* of the sandwich bread. Top with remaining slices. Pack each sandwich in a freezer bag. Store up to 1 month in the freezer. Makes 4 sandwiches.

Don't skip peanut butter sandwiches just because they stick to the roof of your mouth. Try this flavorful concoction! Cream cheese and pineapple add to the flavor and make the peanut butter easier to eat, too.

Lettuce leaves

● For *each* serving, in the morning pack *1* lettuce leaf in a small clear plastic bag. Carry lettuce with *1 frozen* sandwich in a brown bag with a frozen ice pack. The sandwich will thaw in 4 to 6 hours.

At mealtime, add lettuce to sandwich.

Peanut Butter-Sunshine Sandwiches (see recipe, page 13)

Peanutty Baconwiches

½ cup chunk-style peanut
    butter
2 tablespoons mayonnaise
    or salad dressing
1 medium tomato, peeled,
    seeded, and chopped
¼ cup cooked bacon pieces
2 tablespoons sweet pickle
    relish
1 tablespoon finely chopped
    onion (optional)

● In a bowl combine the chunk-style peanut butter and the mayonnaise or salad dressing. Stir to mix well.

Stir in the chopped tomato, cooked bacon pieces, sweet pickle relish, and the finely chopped onion, if desired. Pack in a small airtight container. Store up to 1 week in the refrigerator. Makes enough spread for 3 sandwiches.

Here's a savory peanut butter spread for more sophisticated tastes. Serve it on Tomato-Cheese Bread (see recipe, page 24) or Cheese-Cornmeal Loaf (see recipe, page 29), too. It makes a deliciously extraordinary sandwich.

Sandwich bread

● For *each* serving, in the morning use *⅓ cup chilled* spread and *2 slices* bread to make a sandwich. Pack in a small clear plastic bag. Carry in an insulated lunch box with a frozen ice pack.

Crab-Filled Croissants

Pictured on page 5.

1 **7-ounce can crab meat, drained, flaked, and cartilage removed** ¼ **cup chopped celery** 1 **green onion, thinly sliced**	● In a bowl combine the flaked crab meat, chopped celery, and thinly sliced green onion.
⅓ **cup mayonnaise** *or* **salad dressing** 1 **teaspoon prepared mustard** **Several dashes bottled hot pepper sauce**	● Stir in the mayonnaise or salad dressing, mustard, and hot pepper sauce. Pack in an airtight container. Store up to 1 week in the refrigerator. Makes enough filling for 2 sandwiches.
Croissants, split, *or* **sandwich bread** **Lettuce leaves** **Tomato slices (optional)**	● For *each* serving, in the morning spoon *half* (about ⅔ cup) of the *chilled* mixture into a prechilled insulated vacuum bottle (see tip, page 46). Pack *1* croissant or *2 slices* of bread in a small clear plastic bag. Pack a lettuce leaf and tomato slices, if desired, in separate plastic bags. Carry all in a brown bag. At serving time, assemble croissant or bread, crab filling, lettuce, and, if desired, tomato slices into a sandwich.

Our food editors agreed— this delicately flavored seafood filling layered in a croissant makes an unbeatable lunch. "It's better than eating out!" one declared.

Shrimp Cocktail Pockets

Pictured on page 4.

1 **4½-ounce can shrimp, rinsed and drained** ¼ **cup finely chopped celery** ¼ **cup chopped water chestnuts** 3 **tablespoons Thousand Island salad dressing**	● In a small bowl combine the shrimp, finely chopped celery, chopped water chestnuts, and Thousand Island salad dressing. Toss gently to coat. Pack mixture in a small airtight container. Store up to 1 month in the freezer. Makes enough filling for 1 sandwich.
1 **large pita bread round, split crosswise,** *or* **one croissant, split** **Cucumber slices** *or* **one large lettuce leaf**	● For *1* serving, in the morning pack the pita halves or croissant and the cucumber slices or lettuce in separate small clear plastic bags. Carry with the *frozen* shrimp mixture in a brown bag with a frozen ice pack. At mealtime, assemble the pita halves or croissant, shrimp mixture, and cucumber or lettuce into a sandwich.

One bite was all it took for one of our food editors to exclaim, "An elegant sandwich like this would make other brown baggers jealous!" Stir up the easy filling mixture and taste for yourself.

Creamy Eggs on Rye

2 hard-cooked eggs, chopped
½ cup shredded sharp cheddar cheese (2 ounces)
4 large radishes, chopped (⅓ cup)
½ of a 3-ounce package cream cheese, softened
1 tablespoon milk
⅛ teaspoon salt
Dash pepper

● In a bowl stir together the chopped hard-cooked eggs, shredded sharp cheddar cheese, and chopped radishes. Add the softened cream cheese, milk, salt, and pepper. Stir to mix well. Pack in a small airtight container. Store up to 1 week in the refrigerator. Makes enough spread for 2 sandwiches.

Elaborately layered Danish open-face sandwiches were the inspiration for this unique egg and rye team-up. We've made the packing easier by combining all the ingredients into an easy-to-spread-and-carry filling that goes on a neat-to-eat bun.

Dilly Rye Rolls, split (see recipe, page 29), *or* sandwich bread
Tomato slices (optional)

● For *each* sandwich, spread *half* of the *chilled* egg mixture onto the bottom half of *1* roll or *1 slice* of bread. Top with the remaining roll half or *another slice* of bread. Pack the sandwich in a small clear plastic bag. Pack *2 or 3* tomato slices, if desired, in a separate small clear plastic bag. Carry the sandwich and tomato slices in an insulated lunch box with a frozen ice pack.

At mealtime, add the tomato slices to the sandwich.

Mandarin-Chicken Sandwiches

⅔ cup diced cooked chicken
⅓ cup canned mandarin orange sections, drained and halved
¼ cup chopped cucumber
3 tablespoons creamy cucumber salad dressing
⅛ teaspoon celery seed

● In a bowl combine the diced cooked chicken, halved mandarin orange sections, and chopped cucumber. Add the cucumber salad dressing and celery seed; toss gently to coat. Divide between 2 small airtight containers. Store up to 1 week in the refrigerator. Makes enough filling for 2 sandwiches.

Save lots of calories without sacrificing flavor by using low-calorie or reduced-calorie salad dressings instead of the regular products in these and other sandwiches.

1 large pita bread round, split crosswise
Lettuce leaves

● For *each* serving, in the morning pack *half* of the pita and *1* lettuce leaf in separate small clear plastic bags. Carry with *1 container* of the *chilled* chicken mixture in an insulated lunch box with a frozen ice pack.

At lunchtime, spoon the chicken mixture into the lettuce-lined pita half.

Walnut-Fruit Sandwiches

½ teaspoon finely shredded
    orange peel
½ cup orange juice
¾ cup walnuts
⅓ cup dried apples
⅓ cup pitted dates
⅓ cup raisins

● In a blender container or food processor bowl combine the orange peel and orange juice. Add the walnuts, dried apples, dates, and raisins. Cover and process till nearly smooth, about 2 minutes, stopping to scrape sides, if necessary. Divide mixture between 2 small airtight containers. Store up to 3 weeks in the refrigerator. Makes enough spread for 2 servings.

For hectic days when your appetite demands an extra-filling lunch, pack this richly satisfying walnut butter. Spread it thickly, making two open-face sandwiches at lunchtime.

Whole Wheat-Pecan Loaf (see recipe, page 23) or sandwich bread

● For *each* serving, in the morning pack *2 slices* of bread in a small clear plastic bag. Carry the bread with *1 container* of the walnut mixture in a brown bag.
    At lunchtime, spread *half* of the walnut mixture onto *each* slice of bread.

Mediterranean Sandwiches

1 **15-ounce can garbanzo beans, drained** ¼ **cup tahini (sesame seed paste)** 3 **tablespoons lemon juice** 2 **cloves garlic, minced** ½ **teaspoon salt** ¼ **teaspoon paprika** ½ **cup snipped parsley** 1 **2-ounce jar pimiento, drained and chopped**	● In a blender container or food processor bowl combine the drained garbanzo beans, tahini, lemon juice, garlic, salt, and paprika. Cover and process till smooth, stopping to scrape sides, if necessary. Stir in the snipped parsley and chopped pimiento.	*Pictured on page 5.* **Tahini, or sesame seed paste, is available in Oriental markets and in some large grocery stores.** **Or, you can easily make your own in a blender: Process ½ cup *sesame seed*, covered, in a blender or a food processor fitted with a steel blade until the seed is the consistency of a fine powder. Add 2 tablespoons *cooking oil*. Cover and process till smooth. Makes ¼ cup.**
5 **bagels, split, *or* Herbed Sesame Buns, split (see recipe, page 28)**	● Spread about *⅓ cup* of the mixture onto the bottom half of *each* bagel or bun. Top with the remaining halves. Pack each sandwich in a freezer bag. Store up to 1 month in the freezer. Makes 5 sandwiches.	
	● For *each* serving, in the morning pack *1 frozen* sandwich in a brown bag. Sandwich will thaw at room temperature in 4 to 6 hours.	

Double Cheese-Hamwiches

½ **cup shredded cheddar cheese (2 ounces)** 1 **3-ounce package cream cheese, softened** 2 **teaspoons brown *or* Dijon-style mustard** 1 **2½-ounce package very thinly sliced smoked ham, cut up** 2 **tablespoons chopped sweet pickle *or* sweet pickle relish**	● In a small bowl stir together the shredded cheddar cheese, softened cream cheese, and brown or Dijon-style mustard. Stir in the cut-up smoked ham and chopped sweet pickle or sweet pickle relish.	*Pictured on page 5.* **For a triple-cheese version of this sandwich, try spreading the ham salad mixture on slices of Cheese-Cornmeal Loaf (see recipe, page 29).**
6 **slices sandwich bread**	● Spread *one-third* of the mixture onto each of *3 slices* of bread. Top with remaining slices. Pack each sandwich in a freezer bag. Store up to 1 month in the freezer. Makes 3 sandwiches.	
Lettuce leaves	● For *each* serving, in the morning pack *1 lettuce leaf* in a small clear plastic bag. Carry the lettuce leaf with *1 frozen* sandwich in an insulated lunch box with a frozen ice pack. At mealtime, add the lettuce leaf to the sandwich.	

Sack Lunch Savvy

Veteran brown baggers know that sandwiches are ideal tote-alongs because they're simple to prepare, pack, and eat. Still, it's easy to get stuck in a rut by packing the same sandwich day after day. Break out of that rut by taking advantage of the inventive spread and filling recipes on pages 6-19. You'll find you can make a different sandwich every weekday for a month! And that's not all. Here are more ideas designed to help you take the ho-hum out of bring-your-own lunches.

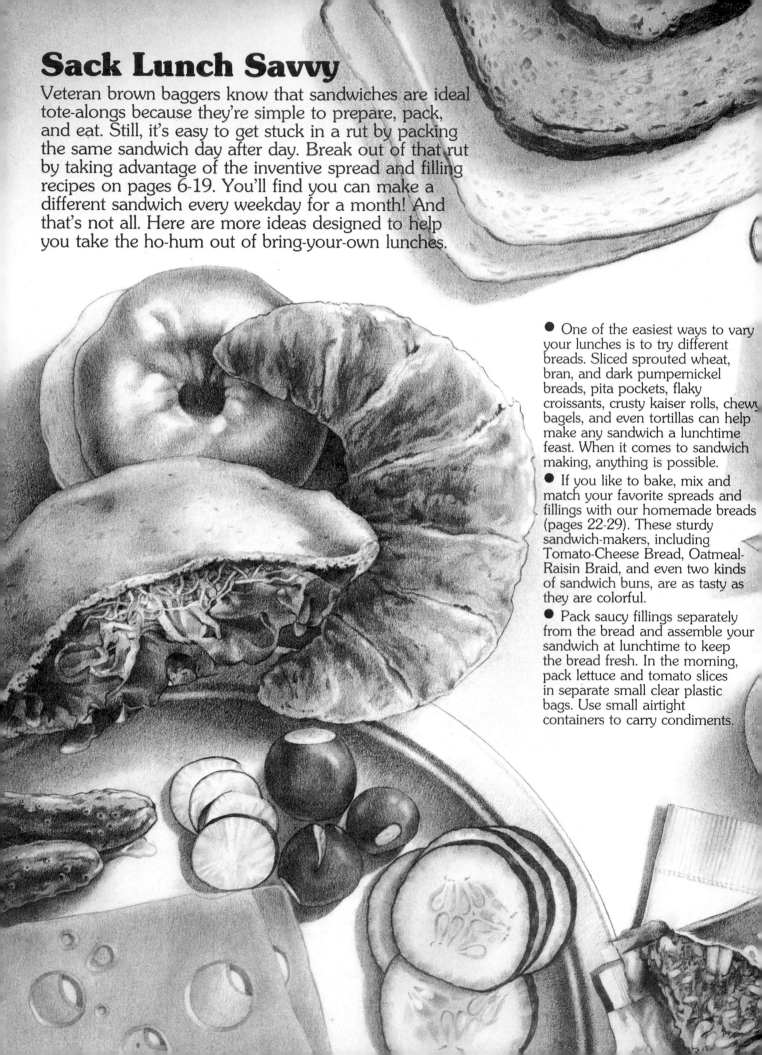

● One of the easiest ways to vary your lunches is to try different breads. Sliced sprouted wheat, bran, and dark pumpernickel breads, pita pockets, flaky croissants, crusty kaiser rolls, chewy bagels, and even tortillas can help make any sandwich a lunchtime feast. When it comes to sandwich making, anything is possible.

● If you like to bake, mix and match your favorite spreads and fillings with our homemade breads (pages 22-29). These sturdy sandwich-makers, including Tomato-Cheese Bread, Oatmeal-Raisin Braid, and even two kinds of sandwich buns, are as tasty as they are colorful.

● Pack saucy fillings separately from the bread and assemble your sandwich at lunchtime to keep the bread fresh. In the morning, pack lettuce and tomato slices in separate small clear plastic bags. Use small airtight containers to carry condiments.

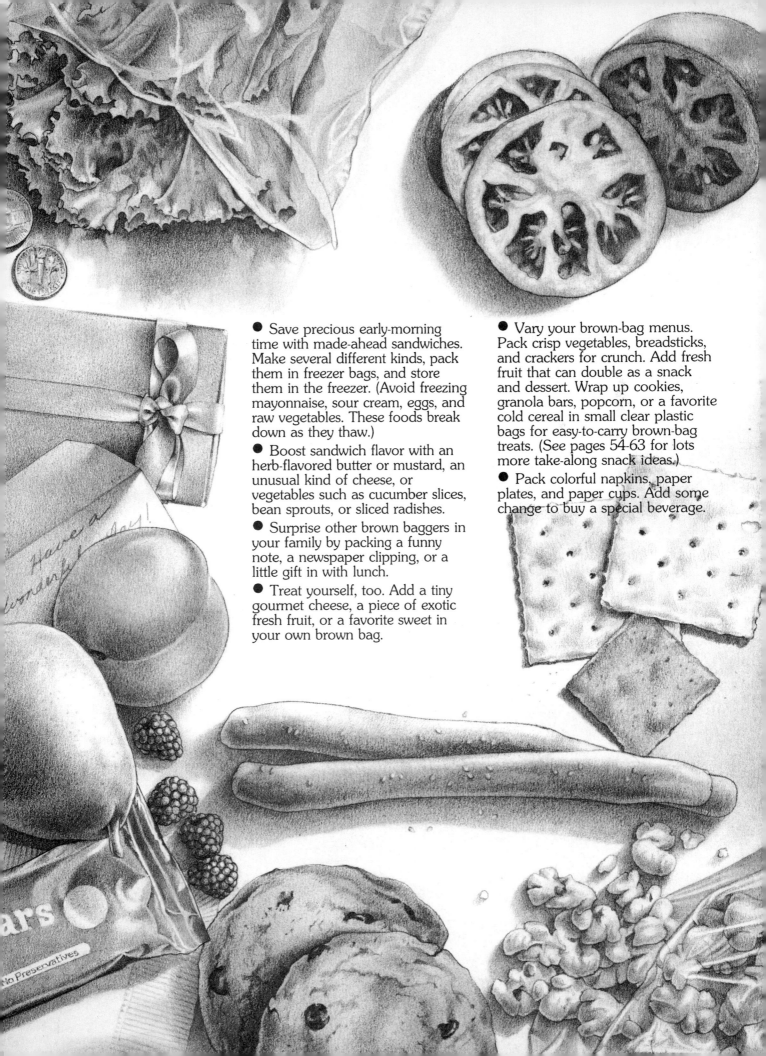

- Save precious early-morning time with made-ahead sandwiches. Make several different kinds, pack them in freezer bags, and store them in the freezer. (Avoid freezing mayonnaise, sour cream, eggs, and raw vegetables. These foods break down as they thaw.)

- Boost sandwich flavor with an herb-flavored butter or mustard, an unusual kind of cheese, or vegetables such as cucumber slices, bean sprouts, or sliced radishes.

- Surprise other brown baggers in your family by packing a funny note, a newspaper clipping, or a little gift in with lunch.

- Treat yourself, too. Add a tiny gourmet cheese, a piece of exotic fresh fruit, or a favorite sweet in your own brown bag.

- Vary your brown-bag menus. Pack crisp vegetables, breadsticks, and crackers for crunch. Add fresh fruit that can double as a snack and dessert. Wrap up cookies, granola bars, popcorn, or a favorite cold cereal in small clear plastic bags for easy-to-carry brown-bag treats. (See pages 54-63 for lots more take-along snack ideas.)

- Pack colorful napkins, paper plates, and paper cups. Add some change to buy a special beverage.

Granana Batter Bread
(see recipe, page 25)

Tomato-Cheese Bread
(see recipe, page 24)

Whole Wheat-Pecan Loaf

Dilly Rye Rolls
(see recipe, page 29)

Cheese-Cornmeal Loaf
(see recipe, page 29)

Sesame Herb Buns
(see recipe, page 28)

Whole Wheat-Pecan Loaf

1½ cups all-purpose flour
½ cup whole wheat flour
½ teaspoon baking soda
½ teaspoon salt

2 eggs
1 cup buttermilk
¼ cup cooking oil
¼ cup packed brown sugar
2 teaspoons finely shredded
　lemon peel
¾ cup finely chopped pecans
　or walnuts

● In a mixing bowl combine the all-purpose flour, whole wheat flour, baking soda, and salt. Stir to mix well. Set aside.

● In another mixing bowl combine the eggs, buttermilk, cooking oil, brown sugar, and finely shredded lemon peel. Beat to mix well.
　Add the flour mixture, stirring just till moistened. Fold in the finely chopped pecans or walnuts.

● Spread batter in a greased 8x4x2-inch loaf pan. Bake in a 350° oven for 50 to 55 minutes or till a toothpick inserted near the center comes out clean. Cool in pan 10 minutes. Remove from pan; cool on a wire rack. Chill overnight before slicing. Makes 1 loaf.

Storing this quick-to-make bread overnight does more than just make the bread easier to slice. The extra storage time also mellows the nutty, lemony flavor so the bread's just right to serve with chicken salad or your favorite nut butters.

Tomato-Cheese Bread

Pictured on page 22.

5½ to 6 cups all-purpose flour 2 packages active dry yeast	● In a large mixer bowl combine *2 cups* of the flour and the yeast.
1 cup tomato juice ¾ cup water 3 tablespoons butter *or* margarine 1½ teaspoons salt 1 egg 1½ cups shredded cheddar *or* American cheese (6 ounces)	● In a saucepan heat the tomato juice, water, butter or margarine, and salt just till warm (115° to 120°) and butter is almost melted. Stir constantly. Add to flour mixture. Add egg and cheese. Beat with an electric mixer on low speed for ½ minute, scraping sides of bowl. Beat on high speed for 3 minutes.
	● With a spoon, stir in as much of the remaining flour as you can. Turn out on a lightly floured surface. Knead in enough of the remaining flour to make a moderately stiff dough (6 to 8 minutes total), as shown at right. Shape into a ball. Place in a greased bowl; turn once. Cover; let the dough rise in a warm place till double (about 1 hour).
Melted shortening Poppy seed (optional)	● Punch dough down. Divide in half. Cover; let rest 10 minutes. Shape into loaves. Place in two greased 8x4x2-inch loaf pans. Cover; let rise till nearly double (about 45 minutes). Brush the tops with shortening and sprinkle with poppy seed, if desired. Bake in a 375° oven for 30 to 40 minutes. Cover with foil the last 15 minutes, if necessary, to prevent overbrowning. Remove from pans; cool on wire rack. Makes 2 loaves.

Kneading helps give bread a smooth, even texture. Knead the dough on a lightly floured surface or on a well-floured pastry cloth. Fold the dough and push it down with the heels of your hands. Give the dough a quarter-turn, then fold it and push it down again. Continue kneading, adding enough of the remaining flour to prevent stickiness, till the dough is moderately stiff and smooth and elastic.

Storing Home-Baked Breads

To keep all your delicious made-from-scratch breads at their best, follow our stay-fresh storage tips:
● Cool breads thoroughly on a wire rack.
● Wrap quick breads in foil; store in the refrigerator up to one week.
● Pack yeast breads in clear plastic bags. Store two to three days at room temperature or up to two weeks in the refrigerator.
● For longer storage, double-wrap quick breads or yeast breads in freezer bags; freeze up to four months.

Granana Batter Bread

Pictured on page 22.

1½ cups all-purpose flour 1 package active dry yeast ½ teaspoon baking soda ¼ teaspoon ground cinnamon	● In a large mixer bowl combine the all-purpose flour, yeast, baking soda, and ground cinnamon. Set aside.

½ cup milk
2 tablespoons brown sugar
2 tablespoons butter *or*
    margarine
¾ teaspoon salt
⅔ cup mashed ripe banana
    (2 medium)
1 egg
	● In a saucepan combine the milk, brown sugar, butter or margarine, and salt. Cook and stir over low heat just till warm (115° to 120°) and butter is almost melted. Add to the flour mixture; add the mashed banana and egg. Beat with an electric mixer on low speed for ½ minute, scraping sides of bowl constantly. Beat on high speed for 3 minutes.

1 cup whole wheat flour ¾ cup granola	● With a spoon, stir in the whole wheat flour and granola to make a soft dough. Cover; let rise in a warm place till double (about 1 hour). Stir down; spread into a greased 8x4x2-inch loaf pan. Cover; let rise in a warm place till nearly double (about 1 hour).
	● Bake in a 375° oven for 30 to 35 minutes or till done. Cover with foil the last 10 minutes to prevent overbrowning. Remove bread from pan; cool completely on a wire rack. Makes 1 loaf.

If your granola is extra chunky, crush the large pieces before stirring the granola into the batter.

For easy crushing, place the granola in a plastic bag. Seal the bag. Use a rolling pin to roll over the closed bag, breaking up the large pieces.

Oatmeal-Raisin Braid

4¼ to 4¾ cups all-purpose
flour
2 packages active dry yeast

● In a large mixer bowl combine *2 cups* of the flour and the yeast.

This moist oat bread nearly bursts with plumped-up raisins. To plump the raisins, place them in a saucepan and cover with water. Bring the mixture to boiling. Remove from heat and let stand five minutes; drain the raisins.

3 tablespoons butter *or*
margarine
2 tablespoons honey
4 teaspoons finely shredded
orange peel
2 teaspoons salt
¼ to ⅓ cup orange juice
(1 orange)

● In a saucepan combine the butter or margarine, honey, finely shredded orange peel, and salt. Add *water* to the orange juice to equal *1¾ cups* liquid. Add the liquid to the mixture in saucepan; heat and stir just till warm (115° to 120°) and butter is almost melted.

Add to the flour mixture. Beat with an electric mixer on low speed for ½ minute, scraping sides of bowl. Beat on high speed for 3 minutes.

1½ cups quick-cooking rolled
oats
1 cup raisins, plumped
(see tip, far right)

● With a spoon, stir in the 1½ cups quick-cooking rolled oats, plumped raisins, and as much of the remaining all-purpose flour as you can. On a lightly floured surface knead in enough of the remaining flour to make a moderately stiff dough that is smooth and elastic (6 to 8 minutes). Shape into a ball. Place in a greased bowl; turn once to grease surface. Cover; let the dough rise in a warm place till double (about 1 hour).

1 beaten egg yolk
1 tablespoon water
Quick-cooking rolled
oats, crushed

● Punch dough down; divide in half. Divide each half into 3 equal pieces. Cover; let rest 10 minutes.

Working with 3 pieces at a time, roll each piece into a 10-inch rope. To make a braid as shown opposite, line up the 3 ropes 1 inch apart. Begin in the middle of the ropes and work toward the ends, braiding loosely. Gently straighten the ropes. Pinch the ends together. Place the braid in a greased 8x4x2-inch loaf pan, tucking ends under. Repeat with the remaining 3 pieces. Cover; let dough rise till nearly double (about 45 minutes).

Beat together the egg yolk and water; brush over the top of each braid. Sprinkle tops with the crushed quick-cooking rolled oats.

● Bake in a 375° oven for 45 to 50 minutes. Cover the loaves with foil the last 15 minutes, if necessary, to prevent overbrowning. Remove the loaves from pans; cool bread completely on a wire rack. Makes 2 loaves.

Sesame Herb Buns

Pictured on page 23.

3½ to 4 cups all-purpose flour
½ cup cornmeal
1 package active dry yeast
1 teaspoon celery seed
1 teaspoon dried basil, crushed
½ teaspoon dried sage, crushed (optional)

● In a large mixer bowl combine *1½ cups* of the flour, the cornmeal, yeast, celery seed, crushed basil, and the crushed sage, if desired.

We recommend these flavorful sandwich buns for our Mediterranean Sandwiches (see recipe, page 19). Because the spread for that sandwich is well seasoned, you'll have plenty of flavor in the sandwich without adding sage to the savory bread dough.

1 cup milk
⅓ cup butter *or* margarine
3 tablespoons sugar
1 teaspoon salt
2 eggs

● In a saucepan heat the milk, butter or margarine, sugar, and salt just till warm (115° to 120°) and butter is almost melted. Add to flour mixture. Add eggs. Beat with an electric mixer on low speed for ½ minute, scraping sides of bowl. Beat on high speed for 3 minutes.

● With a spoon, stir in as much of the remaining flour as you can. On a lightly floured surface, knead in enough of the remaining flour to make a moderately stiff dough that is smooth and elastic (6 to 8 minutes total). Shape into a ball. Place the dough in a greased bowl; turn once to grease surface. Cover; let rise in a warm place till double (about 1 hour).

1 beaten egg yolk
1 tablespoon water
2 to 3 tablespoons sesame seed

● Punch dough down; divide into 12 pieces. Cover; let rest 10 minutes.
  Shape each piece into an even circle or an oval, folding edge under. Press flat between hands. Place each on a greased baking sheet; press into a 3½-inch circle or a 4½-by-2½-inch oval. Cover; let rise till nearly double (about 30 minutes). Brush tops of buns with a mixture of egg yolk and water. Sprinkle sesame seeds atop each bun. Bake in a 375° oven for 15 to 18 minutes or till golden. Remove from baking sheet. Cool completely on a wire rack. Makes 12 buns.

Cheese-Cornmeal Loaf

1 tablespoon cornmeal 3 to 3½ cups all-purpose flour ½ cup cornmeal 2 tablespoons sugar 1 package active dry yeast	● Grease a 1½-quart casserole. Sprinkle with 1 tablespoon cornmeal; set aside. In a large mixer bowl combine *1½ cups* flour, the ½ cup cornmeal, sugar, yeast, and 1 teaspoon *salt*.
1¼ cups warm water (115° to 120°) 2 tablespoons cooking oil 1 egg	● Add the water, cooking oil, and egg. Beat with an electric mixer on low speed for ½ minute, scraping sides of bowl. Beat on high speed for 3 minutes.
1 cup shredded cheddar cheese (4 ounces) ¼ cup snipped parsley	● With a spoon, stir in the cheese, parsley, and as much remaining flour as you can. On a lightly floured surface, knead in enough remaining flour to make a moderately stiff dough (6 to 8 minutes). Place in prepared casserole. Cover; let rise till nearly double (about 1 hour). Bake in a 350° oven for 50 to 60 minutes or till done. Remove from casserole; cool completely. Makes 1 loaf.

Pictured on page 23.

For a big sandwich to satisfy a really robust appetite, cut two slices all the way through this round loaf. For a smaller appetite, use two thin, pie-shaped wedges, or cut a large slice in half to make a sandwich.

Dilly Rye Rolls

Pictured on page 23.

3¼ to 3¾ cups all-purpose flour 2 packages active dry yeast 1½ teaspoons dillseed 1 teaspoon caraway seed	● In a mixer bowl combine *2½ cups* all-purpose flour, the yeast, dillseed, and caraway seed.
1½ cups milk ¼ cup packed brown sugar 3 tablespoons shortening 2 teaspoons salt 2 eggs 2 cups rye flour	● In a saucepan heat milk, brown sugar, shortening, and salt just till warm (115° to 120°). Add to flour mixture; add eggs. Beat with an electric mixer on low speed for ½ minute, scraping sides of bowl. Beat on high speed for 3 minutes. With a spoon, stir in rye flour and as much remaining all-purpose flour as you can. Knead in enough remaining all-purpose flour to make a moderately stiff dough (6 to 8 minutes). Shape into a ball. Place in greased bowl; turn once. Cover; let rise till double (1¼ hours).
1 slightly beaten egg white 1 tablespoon water Coarse salt *or* dillseed (optional)	● Punch down; divide into 12 pieces. Cover; let rest 10 minutes. Shape as directed at right. Let rise, covered, till nearly double (about 1 hour). Brush with mixture of egg white and water. Sprinkle with coarse salt or dillseed, if desired. Bake in a 375° oven for 15 to 20 minutes. Remove from baking sheet. Cool on a wire rack. Makes 12 buns.

Shape each piece of dough into an even circle or an oval, folding edge under. Press flat between hands. Place each piece on a greased baking sheet; press into a 3½-inch circle or a 4½-by-2½-inch oval.

1 As the bread dough rises, make the filling. Toss together the mozzarella cheese, salami, chopped tomato, and Parmesan cheese.

Cheese and Salami Calzones

2 to 2½ cups all-purpose flour
1 package active dry yeast
1 teaspoon dried sage, crushed
½ teaspoon salt
¾ cup warm water (115° to 120°)
2 tablespoons cooking oil

● In large mixer bowl combine *1 cup* flour, the yeast, sage, and salt. Add warm water and oil. Beat with an electric mixer on low speed for ½ minute. Beat on high speed for 3 minutes. Stir in as much of the remaining flour as you can. On a floured surface, knead in enough remaining flour to make a moderately stiff dough that is smooth and elastic (6 to 8 minutes total). Place in a greased bowl; turn once. Cover; let rise in a warm place till double (45 to 55 minutes).

Pack each calzone in a small clear plastic bag or freezer bag. Store up to one week in the refrigerator or up to one month in the freezer. Carry in a brown bag or in an insulated lunch box with a frozen ice pack. (Frozen calzones will thaw in four to six hours.)

1½ cups shredded mozzarella cheese (6 ounces)
⅓ pound salami, chopped
1 small tomato, peeled, seeded, and chopped
⅓ cup grated Parmesan cheese
1 egg
1 teaspoon water

● Meanwhile, make filling. In a bowl toss together the shredded mozzarella cheese, chopped salami, chopped tomato, and grated Parmesan cheese. Set the filling aside. Punch dough down; divide into 6 pieces. Cover; let dough rest 10 minutes.

Roll each piece into a 7-inch circle. Spoon about ½ cup filling onto half of each. Combine egg and water; moisten edges of dough. Fold circle in half; use tines of a fork to seal. Place on greased baking sheet. Prick tops; brush with egg mixture. Bake in a 375° oven for 25 to 30 minutes or till golden. Remove from baking sheet; cool on wire rack. Makes 6.

To make child-size calzones, divide the dough into *12* pieces. Roll each into a *5-inch* circle and fill with about ¼ *cup* of the filling.

2 Punch down the risen dough and divide it into six pieces. Cover the pieces and let rest for 10 minutes.

3 With a rolling pin roll each piece of dough into a 7-inch circle.

4 Spoon about ½ cup of the cheese mixture onto half of each circle of dough. Moisten edges of the dough with a mixture of the egg and water.

5 Fold the circle in half over the filling. Use the tines of a fork to seal the edges together so none of the filling leaks out as the calzones bake.

Spicy Chicken Triangles

1¾ to 2 cups all-purpose
    flour
  1 package active dry yeast
  ½ teaspoon chili powder
  ½ teaspoon salt
  ⅔ cup warm water
    (115° to 120°)
  1 tablespoon cooking oil

● In a small mixer bowl combine ⅔ *cup* of the flour, the yeast, chili powder, and ½ teaspoon salt. Add the warm water and the cooking oil. Beat with an electric mixer on low speed for ½ minute, scraping sides of bowl. Beat on high speed for 3 minutes.

It's a blend of several spicy ingredients that gives these sandwich triangles a just-right hotness. Chili powder goes into the bread dough, which surrounds a cheesy chicken filling seasoned with garlic, coriander, and green chili peppers.

● With a spoon, stir in as much of the remaining flour as you can. On a floured surface knead in enough remaining flour to make a moderately stiff dough that is smooth and elastic (6 to 8 minutes). Shape into a ball. Place in a greased bowl; turn once. Cover and let rise in a warm place till double (about 1 hour).

  ½ cup chopped onion
  ¼ cup chopped green pepper
  1 clove garlic, minced
  ½ teaspoon ground
    coriander
  2 tablespoons butter *or*
    margarine
  2 tablespoons tomato paste
  ¼ teaspoon salt

● Meanwhile, prepare the filling. In a skillet cook the chopped onion, chopped green pepper, minced garlic, and ground coriander in butter or margarine till the onion and green pepper are tender. Stir the tomato paste and ¼ teaspoon salt into the cooked vegetable mixture.

  1 cup chopped cooked
    chicken *or* turkey
  1 8-ounce can whole kernel
    corn, drained
  ½ cup shredded Monterey
    Jack cheese (2 ounces)
  ½ of a 4-ounce can green
    chili peppers, rinsed,
    seeded, and chopped

● In a bowl combine the chopped cooked chicken or turkey, whole kernel corn, shredded Monterey Jack cheese, and green chili peppers. Add the cooked vegetable mixture; stir to mix well. Set the filling aside.

● Punch dough down; divide into 4 pieces. Cover; let rest 10 minutes. Roll each piece into a 6- to 8-inch square. Spoon about ½ *cup* of the filling atop each. Moisten the edges of the dough. Bring 2 opposite corners of each square together to form a triangle. With the tines of a fork, press edges together. Bake on a greased baking sheet in a 375° oven for 25 to 30 minutes. Cool on a wire rack up to 1 hour. Pack each triangle in a freezer bag. Store up to 1 month in the freezer. Makes 4 servings.

● For *each* serving, in the morning pack *1 frozen* sandwich in an insulated lunch box with a frozen ice pack.

Poultry Bundles

1 package (8) refrigerated crescent rolls	● Unroll the crescent rolls; separate into 4 portions. Pinch perforations to seal.
2 5-ounce cans chunk-style chicken *or* turkey, drained and chopped **½ cup shredded cheddar cheese (2 ounces)** **¼ cup snipped dried apricots** **¼ cup chopped pecans** **¼ teaspoon celery seed** **1 3-ounce package cream cheese, softened**	● In a bowl combine the chicken, cheddar cheese, apricots, pecans, and celery seed. Stir in the cream cheese. Spoon *one-fourth* of mixture atop *each* crescent roll rectangle. Bring the corners to the center atop filling; seal all the open edges, as shown at right. (Moisten corners, if necessary.) Place each stuffed, sealed rectangle on a baking sheet. Bake in a 375° oven 12 to 15 minutes or till golden. Cool up to 1 hour on a wire rack. Pack each in a small clear plastic bag or freezer bag. Store up to 1 week in the refrigerator or up to 1 month in the freezer. Makes 4 sandwiches.
	● For *each* serving, in the morning pack *1 chilled* sandwich in an insulated lunch box with a frozen ice pack. (Thaw frozen sandwiches overnight in the refrigerator before packing.)

Here's how to keep the filling from leaking as the sandwich bakes: Top each rectangle of dough with the filling. Moisten the corners with water, if necessary. Bring the edges together atop the filling and pinch all the open edges shut.

Ham and Swiss Packets

1 package (8) refrigerated crescent rolls	● Unroll the crescent rolls; separate into 4 portions. Pinch perforations to seal.
2 tablespoons applesauce **1 tablespoon orange marmalade** **1 cup shredded Swiss *or* cheddar cheese (4 ounces)** **1 cup chopped fully cooked ham**	● In a bowl stir together the applesauce and marmalade. Stir in the cheese and ham. Spoon *one-fourth* of the ham mixture atop *each* crescent roll rectangle. Bring corners to center atop filling; seal all open edges, as shown at right. (Moisten corners, if necessary.) Place each stuffed, sealed rectangle on a baking sheet. Bake in a 375° oven 12 to 15 minutes or till golden. Cool up to 1 hour on a wire rack. Pack each sandwich in a small clear plastic bag or freezer bag. Store up to 1 week in the refrigerator or up to 1 month in the freezer. Makes 4 sandwiches.
	● For *each* serving, in the morning pack *1 chilled* sandwich in an insulated lunch box with a frozen ice pack. (Thaw frozen sandwiches overnight in the refrigerator before packing.)

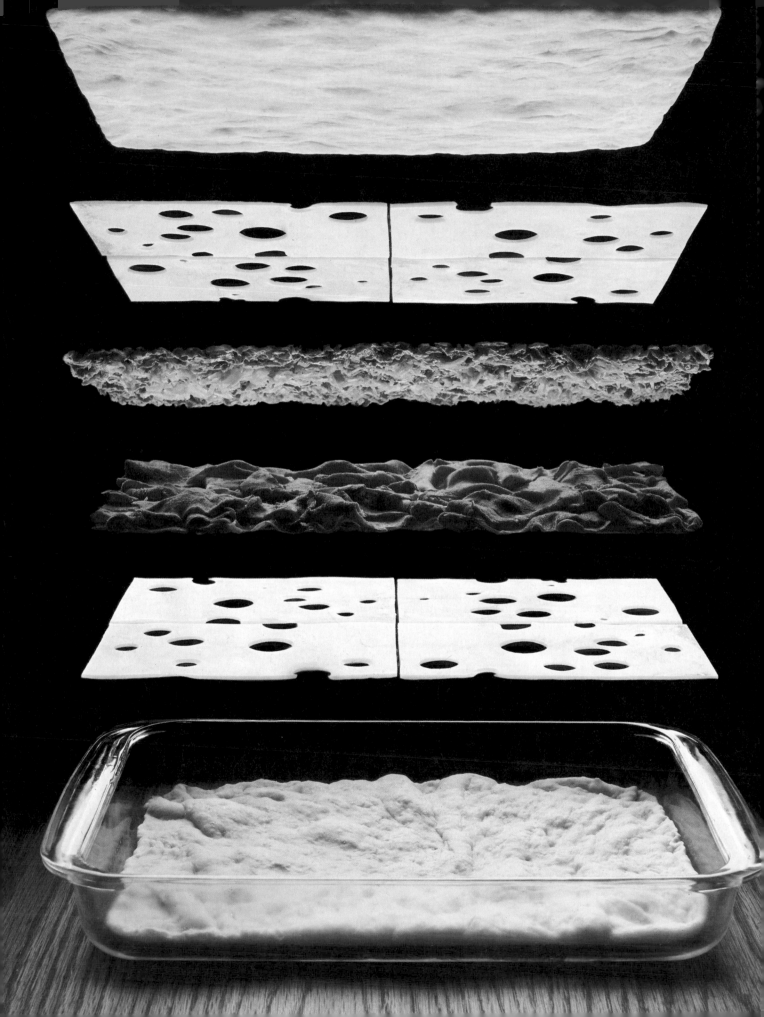

Reuben Sandwich Squares

1 13¾-ounce package hot roll mix

● Prepare hot roll mix according to package directions just through mixing step. Divide dough in half. Let rest, covered, for 10 minutes.

Set aside *1 half* of dough, covered, for top crust. On a lightly floured surface roll the remaining half to a 13x9-inch rectangle. Place in a greased 13x9x2-inch baking dish. Cover; let rise 20 minutes. Bake in a 350° oven for 10 minutes. Remove the dish from the oven. (Baked layer will be lightly golden.)

1 8-ounce can (1 cup) sauerkraut, rinsed and well drained
⅓ cup Thousand Island salad dressing
¼ cup tomato sauce

● Meanwhile, in a small bowl combine the rinsed and drained sauerkraut, Thousand Island salad dressing, and tomato sauce. Stir to mix well. Set the mixture aside.

8 1½-ounce slices Swiss cheese
3 3-ounce packages very thinly sliced corned beef

● Arrange *4 slices* of the cheese over the baked bread layer in the baking dish. Arrange all of the corned beef slices atop the cheese layer. Spoon the sauerkraut mixture over the corned beef. Top with the remaining slices of cheese.

2 teaspoons cooking oil
Caraway seed (optional)

● Roll remaining dough into a 13x9-inch rectangle. Place over corned beef and cheese filling. Crimp edges. Cover; let rest 10 to 15 minutes. Brush the top with cooking oil. Sprinkle lightly with caraway seed, if desired.

Bake in a 350° oven for 30 to 35 minutes or till top is light brown. Cut into 6 squares. Remove each square from the dish and cool up to 1 hour on a wire rack. Pack each cooled square in a freezer bag. Store up to 1 month in the freezer. Makes 6 servings.

● For *each* serving, in the morning pack *1 frozen* sandwich square in a brown bag with a frozen ice pack. The sandwich will thaw in 4 to 6 hours. (*Or,* thaw sandwich overnight in the refrigerator. Carry thawed sandwich in an insulated lunch box with a frozen ice pack.)

One of the first Reubens was a grilled sandwich made with pumpernickel bread. It won a national sandwich contest in the 1950s. Try our winning brown-bag version: It uses a similar filling, this time baked inside white bread to make six satisfying sandwiches at once.

Chicken Liver Pâté

½ pound chicken livers
¼ cup chopped onion
2 tablespoons butter *or* margarine

● In a skillet cook the chicken livers and onion in butter or margarine, covered, about 5 minutes or till the livers are no longer pink, stirring occasionally. Drain, reserving 2 tablespoons of the drippings. Place the liver-onion mixture and reserved drippings in a blender container or food processor bowl. Cover and process till smooth.

⅓ cup finely chopped walnuts *or* pistachio nuts
2 tablespoons mayonnaise *or* salad dressing
1 tablespoon dry sherry *or* dry white wine
¼ teaspoon salt

● In a bowl combine the processed livers and onions, chopped walnuts or pistachio nuts, mayonnaise or salad dressing, sherry or wine, and salt. Stir to mix well. Divide among 4 small freezer containers. Store up to 1 month in the freezer. Makes 4 servings.

● For *each* serving, in the morning, pack *1 container* of *frozen* pâté in an insulated lunch box with a frozen ice pack.

Gourmet takeout doesn't hold a candle to this flavorful yet easy pâté. Take along your favorite crisp crackers or flatbread and a plastic knife for spreading. Add some fresh fruit for dessert.

Pack an Ice Pack

Insulated lunch boxes packed with frozen ice packs will help keep your meal icy cold up to six hours. Use freezer packs designed for coolers; they won't form condensation as they thaw. These blue plastic ice packs are inexpensive, and you can buy them just about anywhere (discount stores, hardware stores, and large grocery stores). Put your ice pack into the freezer the night before so that it's frozen solid when you add it to your lunch box.

Blue Cheese and Beef Loaf

1 beaten egg ⅓ cup tomato juice ¼ cup quick-cooking rolled oats 2 tablespoons finely chopped onion 2 tablespoons snipped parsley 1 teaspoon Worcestershire sauce ¼ teaspoon salt Dash pepper	● In a bowl combine the beaten eggs and tomato juice. Add the quick-cooking rolled oats, finely chopped onion, snipped parsley, Worcestershire sauce, salt, and pepper. Stir to mix well.	**You probably know that cold meat loaf tastes great inside a sandwich. Instead of sandwiching these tangy meat loaf slices between bread, however, we've topped them with a refreshing cucumber sauce to make a special lunch you eat with a fork.**
1 pound lean ground beef ¼ cup crumbled blue cheese (1 ounce)	● Add the ground beef and crumbled blue cheese; mix well. Pat mixture into a 7½x3½x2-inch loaf pan. Bake in a 350° oven for 1 to 1¼ hours. Remove meat loaf from the pan. Cut into 4 to 6 slices. Cool on a wire rack up to 1 hour. Pack each slice in an airtight container or freezer container. Store slices up to 1 week in the refrigerator or up to 1 month in the freezer. Makes 4 to 6 servings.	
Cucumber Sauce (see recipe, below)	● For *each* serving, in the morning spoon 3 to 4 tablespoons Cucumber Sauce over 1 *chilled slice* of beef loaf in the airtight container. Carry in an insulated lunch box with a frozen ice pack. (Thaw frozen slice overnight in the refrigerator before packing.)	

Cucumber Sauce

1 cup plain yogurt ½ cup shredded cucumber ¼ teaspoon onion salt	● In a small bowl combine the plain yogurt, shredded cucumber, and onion salt. Stir till well mixed. Pack the mixture in a small airtight container. Store the sauce up to 1 week in the refrigerator. Makes about 1½ cups sauce.	**Spread this cool sauce on your favorite meat-and-cheese sandwiches, too. Carry the sauce in a small airtight container, then add it at lunchtime.**

Ham 'n' Cheese-Stuffed Chicken Breasts

1 whole large chicken breast, skinned, halved lengthwise, and boned	● Working with one piece at a time, place the chicken, boned side up, between two pieces of clear plastic wrap. Pound out from the center with a meat mallet to ⅛- to ¼-inch thickness, as shown at top right. Remove plastic wrap.

Place the meat between two pieces of clear plastic wrap. Using the flat side of a meat mallet, pound lightly, forming a rectangle ⅛ to ¼ inch thick.

½ of a 3-ounce package cream cheese, softened ¼ cup diced fully cooked ham ¼ cup shredded Swiss cheese (1 ounce) 2 tablespoons finely chopped walnuts ½ teaspoon Dijon-style mustard Dash onion powder	● In a small bowl combine the softened cream cheese, diced ham, shredded Swiss cheese, chopped walnuts, Dijon-style mustard, and onion powder. Stir till well mixed. Spread *each* chicken piece with *half* of the ham mixture, pressing the mixture with the flat edge of a knife, as shown at center right. Fold in the sides of each chicken piece and roll up jelly-roll style, starting from one of the shorter ends, as shown at bottom right. Fasten the chicken rolls with wooden toothpicks.

Use the flat edge of a knife to press *half* (about ¼ cup) of the ham mixture over the top of each chicken piece.

1 tablespoon fine dry bread crumbs 1 teaspoon snipped parsley 2 tablespoons butter *or* margarine, melted	● In a bowl combine the bread crumbs and parsley. Lightly brush the chicken with melted butter or margarine; sprinkle with the crumb mixture. Bake in a shallow baking pan in a 350° oven for 40 to 45 minutes. Cool on a wire rack up to 1 hour.

	● Cover and chill the cooked chicken breasts in the refrigerator for 2 to 3 hours. (*Or,* chill in the freezer for 1 hour.) Then, slice each chilled chicken breast into ¼-inch-thick slices. Pack each group of slices in a separate freezer bag; store up to 1 month in the freezer. Makes 2 servings.

Roll up each chicken piece, jelly-roll style, pressing edges together to enclose the filling. Fasten with wooden toothpicks.

	● For *each* serving, in the morning pack *1 package* of the *frozen* chicken breast slices in an insulated lunch box with a frozen ice pack.

Dilled Tuna Casserole

1 cup water
1 cup loose-pack frozen mixed vegetables
¾ cup quick-cooking rice
½ of an 11-ounce can condensed cheddar cheese soup
1 3¼-ounce can tuna, drained and flaked
1 tablespoon minced dried onion
¼ teaspoon dried dillweed

● In a saucepan combine the water, mixed vegetables, quick-cooking rice, cheddar cheese soup, tuna, minced dried onion, and dillweed. Cook and stir just to boiling; reduce heat. Cover and simmer the mixture about 3 minutes or till the vegetables are nearly tender. Divide mixture between 2 small airtight containers. Store up to 1 week in the refrigerator. Makes 2 servings.

This tasty one-dish meal goes together in less than 20 minutes, so you can even make it in the morning. Simmer the mixture for *five* minutes, or till the vegetables are tender. Then pack in an insulated vacuum bottle as directed.

● For *each* serving, in the morning reheat mixture from *1 container* in a small saucepan. Cook, covered, over medium heat till bubbly. Cook 3 to 5 minutes more, stirring occasionally. (Add a little water if the mixture is dry.) Pack in a preheated insulated vacuum bottle (see tip, page 46).

Curried Lime Chicken

1 small cooking apple, peeled, cored, and chopped
⅓ cup chopped onion
1 clove garlic, minced
1 teaspoon curry powder
1 tablespoon cooking oil

● In a medium saucepan cook the chopped apple, chopped onion, minced garlic, and curry powder in hot cooking oil till the onion is tender but not brown. Set the apple-onion mixture aside.

Brown-bag hot lunches need extra cooking time to keep them hot enough all morning. That's why you need to gently boil the mixture for 3 to 5 minutes. The longer cooking time may make the rice in this dish a little softer than you are used to.

1¼ cups cold water
1 tablespoon cornstarch
1 tablespoon lime juice
1 teaspoon instant chicken bouillon granules

● In a small bowl combine the cold water and cornstarch; stir into the cooked apple-onion mixture. Add the lime juice and chicken bouillon granules. Cook and stir till thickened and bubbly.

1 cup chopped cooked chicken
¾ cup cooked rice
2 tablespoons peanuts
2 tablespoons raisins

● Stir in the chicken, rice, peanuts, and raisins. Divide mixture between 2 small airtight containers. Store up to 1 week in the refrigerator. Makes 2 servings.

● For *each* serving, in the morning reheat mixture from *1 container* in a small saucepan. Cook, covered, over medium heat till bubbly. Cook 3 to 5 minutes longer, stirring occasionally. (Add a little water if mixture is dry.) Pack in a preheated insulated vacuum bottle (see tip, page 46).

Scotch Eggs

1 tablespoon snipped
    parsley
½ pound bulk pork sausage
4 hard-cooked eggs, peeled

● In a bowl stir the parsley into the sausage. Divide the sausage into 4 pieces. Shape each piece into a 4-inch-round patty. Wrap each sausage patty around 1 hard-cooked egg, covering the egg completely.

Here's an easy way to pack eggs and sausage into a take-along lunch. Scotch Eggs are neat to eat; you won't even need a fork. They're great for breakfast, too.

¼ cup all-purpose flour
1 beaten egg
8 rich round cheese
    crackers, crushed
    (⅓ cup)

● Roll each sausage-wrapped egg in the flour. Roll in the beaten egg, then in cracker crumbs. Bake in a shallow baking pan in a 375° oven for 25 to 30 minutes or till sausage is thoroughly cooked. Remove from pan; cool on a wire rack up to 1 hour. Pack each egg in a small clear plastic bag. Store up to 1 week in the refrigerator. Makes 4 servings.

● For *each* serving, pack *1 chilled* Scotch Egg in an insulated lunch box with a frozen ice pack.

1 Divide the sausage mixture into four pieces. With your hands, flatten each piece into a 4-inch-round patty.

2 Wrap each sausage patty around 1 peeled hard-cooked egg, pinching the sausage together to cover the egg completely.

3 After rolling each sausage-wrapped egg in flour and beaten egg, roll it in the cracker crumbs.

4 Arrange the sausage-wrapped and crumb-coated eggs in a shallow baking pan and bake.

5 Transfer the baked Scotch Eggs from the baking pan to a wire rack. Allow to cool up to one hour before packing and storing in the refrigerator.

Chicken-Vegetable Soup

1 8-ounce can cream-style corn
1 7½-ounce can tomatoes, cut up
½ cup carrots, cut into ¼-inch-thick pieces
¼ cup chopped onion
1 tablespoon instant chicken bouillon granules
1 teaspoon dried thyme, crushed
¼ teaspoon pepper
½ cup uncooked medium noodles (1 ounce)
½ cup loose pack frozen cut green beans
1½ cups chopped cooked chicken

● In a saucepan combine 2½ cups *water,* the cream-style corn, *undrained* cut-up tomatoes, carrot pieces, chopped onion, chicken bouillon granules, thyme, and pepper. Cook and stir just to boiling.

Stir in the noodles. Reduce heat. Cover; simmer 5 minutes. Stir in the frozen cut green beans. Cook 3 to 5 minutes more or till vegetables and noodles are tender. Stir in the chicken.

Divide among 4 airtight containers or freezer containers. Store up to 1 week in the refrigerator or up to 1 month in the freezer. Makes 4 (1¼-cup) servings.

Soup is the perfect packable meal for chilly days. One taste of this thick, chunky chicken soup will convince you that it really is worth the effort to make your own.

● For *each* serving, in the morning reheat soup from *1 container* before packing in a preheated insulated vacuum bottle (see tip, page 46).

Chunky Chili

1 pound beef round steak, cut into ¾-inch cubes
1 cup chopped onion
¾ cup chopped green pepper
1 clove garlic, minced
2 tablespoons cooking oil

● In a 3-quart saucepan cook the beef steak cubes, chopped onion, chopped green pepper, and minced garlic in hot cooking oil till the meat is brown. Drain off the fat.

1 16-ounce can tomatoes, cut up
1 cup tomato juice
2 teaspoons paprika
1 teaspoon dried oregano, crushed
½ teaspoon cumin seed, crushed
¼ teaspoon ground red pepper
1 16-ounce can red kidney beans, drained
1 4-ounce can green chili peppers, rinsed, seeded, and chopped

● Add the *undrained* tomatoes, tomato juice, and 1 cup *water* to the saucepan with the beef. Stir in the paprika, oregano, cumin seed, ground red pepper, and ¼ teaspoon *salt.* Bring to boiling. Reduce heat; simmer, covered, about 1¼ hours or till the meat is nearly tender.

Stir in the red kidney beans and chili peppers. Simmer, covered, 15 to 20 minutes more. Divide the mixture among 4 to 6 airtight containers or freezer containers. Store up to 1 week in the refrigerator or up to 1 month in the freezer. Makes 4 to 6 servings.

Pack crunchy bread sticks or crackers when this spicy (but not fiery) chili is on your brown-bag menu. For make-your-own bread sticks, try easy Poppy Seed Twists (see recipe, page 73).

● For *each* serving, in the morning reheat chili from *1 container* before packing in a preheated insulated vacuum bottle (see tip, page 46).

Curried Pork Stew

1 small apple, cored and
   chopped
¼ cup sliced carrots
2 tablespoons chopped
   onion
2 teaspoons curry powder
2 tablespoons butter *or*
   margarine

● In a saucepan cook the chopped apple, sliced carrots, chopped onion, and curry powder in butter or margarine till the onion is tender.

Watch out when you open your insulated bottle if it's full of this rich-tasting stew—the irresistible aromas may lead hungry friends straight to you and your lunch!

1 10¾-ounce can
   condensed tomato soup
1 cup milk
¼ cup raisins
2 tablespoons snipped
   parsley
1½ cups finely chopped
   cooked pork
1 8-ounce carton plain
   yogurt

● Stir in the soup, milk, raisins, and parsley. Add pork; simmer, uncovered, 10 minutes. Stir in yogurt. Divide mixture among 4 small airtight containers or freezer containers. Store stew up to 1 week in the refrigerator or up to 1 month in the freezer. Makes 4 (1-cup) servings.

● For *each* serving, in the morning reheat stew from *1 container* before packing in a preheated insulated vacuum bottle (see tip, page 46).

Ham and Lentil Stew

¾ cup dry lentils
4 cups cold water
1 16-ounce can tomatoes,
   cut up
1 medium onion, cut in
   wedges
2 cloves garlic, minced
¾ teaspoon dried oregano,
   crushed
⅛ teaspoon pepper
1½ cups finely chopped fully
   cooked ham

● Rinse the lentils. In a large saucepan combine the lentils, water, *undrained* tomatoes, onion wedges, minced garlic, crushed oregano, and pepper. Bring mixture to boiling; reduce heat. Cover and simmer 30 minutes.

   Stir in the ham; simmer 5 minutes longer. Divide mixture among 4 small airtight containers or freezer containers. Store up to 1 week in the refrigerator or up to 1 month in the freezer. Makes 4 (1⅔-cup) servings.

Lentils, unlike dried beans, require no presoaking or precooking, so you can make this robust meal-in-one even on busy days. Add some rye crackers to your brown bag to eat with the flavorful stew.

● For *each* serving, in the morning reheat stew from *1 container* before packing in a preheated insulated vacuum bottle (see tip, page 46).

Quick Corn Chowder

1½ cups milk
½ of an 11-ounce can condensed cheddar cheese soup (⅔ cup)
1 8-ounce can whole kernel corn, drained
2 tablespoons packaged instant mashed potatoes
½ of a 2½-ounce package very thinly sliced dried beef, cut up

● In a saucepan combine the milk and soup. Stir in the corn and potatoes. Add the dried beef. (For a less salty taste, rinse the beef before adding to the saucepan.) Cook and stir till hot and bubbly. Divide mixture between 2 small airtight containers or freezer containers. Store up to 1 week in the refrigerator or up to 1 month in the freezer. Makes 2 (1½-cup) servings.

● For *each* serving, in the morning reheat soup from *1 container* before packing in a preheated insulated vacuum bottle (see tip, page 46).

Use the remaining half-can of soup in Dilled Tuna Casserole (see recipe, page 39) for two more quick brown-bag meals.

Manhattan Clam Chowder

1 6½-ounce can minced clams

● Drain the clams, reserving the liquid. Add enough *water* to the reserved liquid to measure 1½ cups.

2 slices bacon, cut up
⅓ cup chopped green pepper
⅓ cup chopped onion

● In a saucepan partially cook bacon. Stir in green pepper and onion; cook till tender. Stir in clam liquid-water mixture.

1 7½-ounce can tomatoes, cut up
1 small potato, diced (⅔ cup)
¼ cup sliced carrots
2 tablespoons catsup
½ bay leaf
¼ teaspoon dried thyme, crushed
⅛ teaspoon salt
Dash pepper

● Stir in the *undrained* tomatoes, diced potato, carrots, catsup, bay leaf, thyme, salt, and pepper. Bring to boiling; reduce heat. Cover and simmer 30 to 35 minutes or till vegetables are tender. Remove bay leaf. With a fork, mash vegetables slightly, as shown at right. Stir in clams; heat through. Divide between 2 small airtight containers or freezer containers. Store chowder up to 1 week in the refrigerator or up to 1 month in the freezer. Makes 2 (1½-cup) servings.

● For *each* serving, in the morning reheat chowder from *1 container* before packing in a preheated insulated vacuum bottle (see tip, page 46).

To thicken the chowder, mash the potatoes and carrots after cooking. Use the back of a fork, pressing the vegetables against the side of the saucepan.

Taco-Potato Soup

2 cups milk
1 10¾-ounce can condensed cream of potato soup
1 tablespoon minced dried onion
⅛ teaspoon garlic powder

● In a saucepan combine the milk, condensed cream of potato soup, minced dried onion, and garlic powder. Cook and stir over medium heat till the mixture is bubbly.

Stir in chili peppers and cheese to give a favorite canned soup Mexican flavor. Then, at lunchtime, sprinkle crispy taco chips over the soup.

1 cup shredded Monterey Jack cheese (4 ounces)
¼ cup chopped canned green chili peppers

● Stir in the shredded Monterey Jack cheese and chopped green chili peppers. Cook and stir till cheese melts.
   Divide among 4 small airtight containers or freezer containers. Store soup up to 1 week in the refrigerator or up to 1 month in the freezer. Makes 4 (1-cup) servings.

Taco chips, broken

● For *each* serving, in the morning reheat soup from *1 container* before packing in a preheated insulated vacuum bottle (see tip, below). Pack taco chips in a small clear plastic bag. Carry with the bottle of soup in a brown bag.
   At lunchtime, sprinkle the taco chips over the soup.

Reheating Soups and Stews

Follow these easy directions to make sure the soup or stew you pour from your vacuum bottle is just the right temperature. First, get it good and hot before you pack it. If the soup is frozen, thaw one or more servings overnight in the refrigerator. In the morning, place the soup in a small saucepan and cover; heat over medium heat, stirring occasionally, till entire surface is bubbly. Cook 3 to 5 minutes more, adding a little more water if necessary. Immediately pour into a preheated insulated vacuum bottle (see tip below).

Keep It Hot or Cold

The secret to *keeping* foods really hot or cold in an insulated vacuum bottle is preheating or prechilling the bottle. To preheat (or prechill), fill the insulated vacuum bottle with hottest (or coldest) tap water. Cover with the lid; let stand 5 minutes. Empty the bottle, shaking out excess moisture. Immediately fill with the hot (or cold) food.

Mideastern Lamb Stew

¾ **pound boneless lamb** *or*
 beef stew meat, cut into
 ¾-inch cubes
2 **tablespoons olive oil** *or*
 cooking oil

● In a large saucepan cook the lamb or
beef stew meat cubes in hot olive oil or
cooking oil till the meat is brown. Drain
off the fat.

**Make your menu
authentic—pack pita
bread cut into wedges
instead of crackers to
dunk into this exotic,
savory stew.**

2 **cups water**
1 **10½-ounce can**
 condensed beef broth
¼ **cup sliced celery**
¼ **cup chopped onion**
1 **clove garlic, minced**
1 **teaspoon ground**
 coriander
¼ **teaspoon ground cumin**
⅛ **teaspoon ground**
 cinnamon
1 **15-ounce can garbanzo**
 beans, drained
½ **cup sliced carrots**

● Add the water, condensed beef broth,
sliced celery, chopped onion, minced
garlic, ground coriander, ground cumin,
and ground cinnamon. Bring to boiling;
reduce heat. Cover; simmer for 1 hour,
stirring occasionally.

Stir in the garbanzo beans and sliced
carrots. Cover; simmer about 25 minutes
more or till meat and carrots are tender.

Divide the stew among 4 small airtight
containers or freezer containers. Store
the stew up to 1 week in the refrigerator
or up to 1 month in the freezer. Makes
4 (1-cup) servings.

● For *each* serving, in the morning
reheat stew from *1 container* before
packing in a preheated insulated vacuum
bottle (see tip, opposite).

Chicken Tabouleh

⅓ cup bulgur wheat	● Place the bulgur in a strainer. Rinse with cold water. Drain well.
1 cup cubed cooked chicken 1 small tomato, peeled, seeded, and chopped ½ cup snipped parsley ¼ cup chopped cucumber 2 tablespoons chopped onion 2 tablespoons sliced radishes	● In a medium bowl combine the rinsed and drained bulgur, cubed cooked chicken, chopped tomato, snipped parsley, chopped cucumber, chopped onion, and sliced radishes. Toss to mix well. Set the mixture aside.
¼ cup olive oil *or* salad oil ¼ cup lemon juice 1 clove garlic, minced ¼ teaspoon salt ⅛ teaspoon pepper	● In a screw-top jar combine the olive or salad oil, lemon juice, garlic, salt, and pepper. Shake well. Pour over bulgur mixture. Toss gently to coat. Pack in an airtight container. Store up to 1 week in the refrigerator. Makes 2 servings.
	● For *each* serving, in the morning pack *half* of the *chilled* chicken and bulgur mixture in a prechilled insulated vacuum bottle (see tip, page 46).

Tabouleh is a traditional Mideastern salad that's made with bulgur wheat. The wheat soaks up its savory dressing as the salad chills overnight. By morning, the grains of bulgur will be plump, tender, and full of flavor.

Spiced Rice and Beef Salad

1 **cup cooked brown rice**	● In a bowl combine the cooked brown rice, chopped cooked beef, raisins, and pine nuts or slivered almonds. Toss to mix well. Set the mixture aside.
¾ **cup chopped cooked beef**	
¼ **cup raisins**	
2 **tablespoons pine nuts** *or* **slivered almonds**	
3 **tablespoons salad oil**	● For dressing, in a small bowl stir together the salad oil, lemon juice, ground cinnamon, ground ginger, ground nutmeg, and onion salt. Add to the rice mixture; toss gently to coat.
1 **tablespoon lemon juice**	
¼ **teaspoon ground cinnamon**	
⅛ **teaspoon ground ginger**	Divide the mixture between 2 small airtight containers. Store up to 1 week in the refrigerator. Makes 2 servings.
⅛ **teaspoon ground nutmeg**	
⅛ **teaspoon onion salt**	
	● For *each* serving, in the morning pack *1 container* of the *chilled* beef and rice mixture in an insulated lunch box with a frozen ice pack.

Our Test Kitchen home economists found that when they first added the dressing, the salad looked a little wet. As the salad chilled overnight, however, the rice and beef mixture absorbed the extra dressing.

Artichoke and Pasta Salad

1 **6-ounce jar marinated artichoke hearts**	● Drain the artichoke hearts, reserving the marinade.
1 **cup cooked corkscrew** *or* **elbow macaroni**	● In a medium bowl combine the drained artichoke hearts, cooked corkscrew or elbow macaroni, cheddar cheese cubes, chopped cucumber, and sliced green onion. Toss to mix well.
4 **ounces cheddar cheese, cut into ½-inch cubes**	
¼ **cup chopped cucumber**	
1 **green onion, sliced**	
½ **cup mayonnaise** *or* **salad dressing**	● For the dressing, in a bowl combine the reserved artichoke marinade and the mayonnaise or salad dressing. Stir to mix well. Pour over the cheese and macaroni mixture; toss gently to coat. Divide the mixture between 2 small airtight containers. Store up to 1 week in the refrigerator. Makes 2 servings.
	● For *each* serving, in the morning pack *1 container* of the *chilled* artichoke and pasta mixture in an insulated lunch box with a frozen ice pack.

When you chill this salad more than one day, you may need to make it moister. If so, stir in a little milk.

Curried Beef on Spinach

1 **medium orange, peeled and sectioned** 1 **cup cubed cooked roast beef** *or* **cooked chicken** ½ **cup seedless grapes, halved** ½ **cup strawberries, halved** 2 **tablespoons sliced celery**	● In a bowl combine the orange sections, cubed cooked beef or cooked chicken, grape halves, strawberry halves, and sliced celery. Toss to mix well. Set the mixture aside.	**You can keep fresh spinach crisp all morning in an insulated lunch box. Just be sure the plastic bag of spinach does not touch the frozen ice pack when you pack your lunch.**
½ **of an 8-ounce carton orange yogurt** 1 **tablespoon milk** ½ **to 1 teaspoon curry powder**	● In another bowl stir together the yogurt, milk, and curry powder. Add to the beef mixture. Toss gently to coat. Divide between 2 small airtight containers. Store the mixture up to 1 week in the refrigerator. Makes enough for 2 servings.	
Torn fresh spinach	● For *each* serving, in the morning pack desired amount of spinach in a small clear plastic bag. Pack with *1 container* of the *chilled* beef mixture in an insulated lunch box with a frozen ice pack. Add a paper plate, napkin, fork, and spoon. At serving time, place spinach on paper plate; spoon beef mixture atop.	

Ham and Potato Salad

¾ **cup fully cooked ham, cut into thin bite-size strips** ¾ **cup cubed cooked potatoes** ¼ **cup chopped cucumber** 2 **tablespoons sliced green onion** 2 **tablespoons chopped pimiento**	● In a small bowl combine the bite-size ham strips, cubed potatoes, chopped cucumber, sliced green onion, and chopped pimiento. Toss to mix well. Set the mixture aside.	**Keep lunch packing easy—find little hide- aways in your office for stashing paper plates, and plastic forks, knives, and spoons.**
⅓ **cup mayonnaise** *or* **salad dressing** ½ **teaspoon sugar** ½ **teaspoon Dijon-style mustard** ¼ **teaspoon garlic salt** ⅛ **teaspoon dried dillweed (optional)**	● In another bowl stir together the mayonnaise or salad dressing, sugar, mustard, garlic salt, and dillweed, if desired. Add the mayonnaise mixture to the ham-potato mixture. Toss gently to coat. Divide the salad between 2 small airtight containers. Store up to 1 week in the refrigerator. Makes 2 servings.	
	● For *each* serving, in the morning pack *1 container* of the *chilled* Ham and Potato Salad in an insulated lunch box with a frozen ice pack.	

Shrimp and Corn Salad

1 **8-ounce can whole kernel corn, drained**
1 **4½-ounce can tiny shrimp, rinsed and drained**
1 **small tomato, peeled, seeded, and chopped**
2 **tablespoons finely chopped onion**
2 **tablespoons snipped parsley**

● In a medium bowl combine the whole kernel corn, rinsed and drained tiny shrimp, chopped tomato, finely chopped onion, and snipped parsley. Toss to mix well. Set aside.

Dare to be different for lunch—toss together our cool and colorful shrimp salad. Then, fill your brown bag with wheat crackers and carrot sticks, and a Raisin Spice Cupcake for dessert (see recipe, page 57).

¼ **cup dairy sour cream**
2 **tablespoons chili sauce**

● For dressing, in a small bowl stir together the sour cream and chili sauce. Add to the corn and shrimp mixture. Toss to coat. Pack in an airtight container. Store up to 1 week in the refrigerator. Makes 2 servings.

● For *each* serving, in the morning pack *half* of the *chilled* corn and shrimp mixture in a prechilled insulated vacuum bottle (see tip, page 46).

Ham-Orange Slaw

1 **cup shredded cabbage**
1 **cup diced fully cooked ham**
1 **6-ounce package frozen pea pods, thawed and halved crosswise**
1 **orange, peeled and sectioned**
¼ **cup chopped green *or* sweet red pepper**
2 **to 4 tablespoons creamy cucumber salad dressing**

● In a bowl combine the shredded cabbage, diced fully cooked ham, halved pea pods, orange sections, and chopped green or red pepper.
 Divide mixture between 2 small airtight containers. Drizzle *1 to 2 tablespoons* of the cucumber salad dressing over the ham and vegetable mixture in each container, as shown at right. Store up to 3 days in the refrigerator. Makes 2 servings.

● For *each* serving, in the morning pack *1 container* of the *chilled* ham and vegetable mixture in an insulated lunch box with a frozen ice pack.
 At lunchtime, toss gently to coat the salad with dressing.

Make sure each of the two servings gets its share of salad dressing. Pour on the dressing *after* dividing the ham and vegetable mixture between two airtight containers.

Thurs
Call Steve

Sack a Salad

In additi... ...ads, you can create your... ...re are some hints to help you ge...

Choose the Vegetables

● Start with one or mo... ...ne many leafy greens such as iceberg or Bibb lettuce; escarole, Swiss chard, or romaine; fresh spinach; or cabbage. Chop or tear the greens into bite-sized pieces. Then add as many other vegetables as you like. Cut strips of green or sweet red pepper. Cut wedges of tomato. Cut thin slices of onion, radish, zucchini, cucumber, or carrots. Chop broccoli or cauliflower into flowerets. Take bean or alfalfa sprouts, if you like, or add chopped olives.

Add Some Protein

● Take along canned tuna, crab meat, salmon, shrimp, chicken, or turkey, or a small package of very thinly sliced chicken, ham, turkey, corned beef, or pastrami. Or, choose cut-up salami, left-over cooked chicken, or roast beef. Or, try sliced or chopped hard-cooked eggs, cheese cubes or strips, or garbanzo beans.

Pack and Carry

● Use plastic bags for wrapping the salad ingredients, packing the juicy ones separately. Put your choice of protein and croutons, if desired, into plastic bags or airtight containers. Pour your favorite dressing into a tiny airtight container. Carry everything in an insulated lunch box with a frozen ice pack. Be sure to include a paper bowl or plate and a plastic fork. Then, come lunchtime, toss and enjoy!

Frosty Fruit Medley

1 **8-ounce can pineapple chunks (juice pack)**
½ **cup walnut halves**
2 **tablespoons orange juice**
¼ **teaspoon ground ginger**
3 **cups fresh *or* frozen strawberries, halved**
1 **cup fresh *or* frozen blueberries**
¼ **cup coconut**

● In a large bowl combine the *undrained* pineapple chunks, walnut halves, orange juice, and ground ginger. Stir to mix well. Add the strawberry halves, blueberries, and coconut. Toss gently to coat the fruit with juice.

Divide the mixture among 4 small airtight containers, leaving extra space for the mixture to expand as it freezes. Store up to 1 month in the freezer. Makes 4 servings.

● For *each* serving, in the morning pack *1 container* of the *frozen* mixture in an insulated lunch box with a frozen ice pack. The fruit mixture will thaw slightly (but remain frosty) in 4 to 6 hours.

When every calorie counts, let this luscious fruit-and-nut combination double for a snack and dessert. Its icy goodness will make you forget you're dieting.

Fruity Flip

1 **small banana, sliced**
1 **cup cranberry juice cocktail**
⅓ **cup orange juice**

● In a blender container or food processor bowl combine the banana slices, cranberry juice cocktail, and orange juice. Cover and process till smooth. Pour mixture into an airtight container. Store up to 3 days in the refrigerator. Makes 2 (1-cup) servings.

● For *each* serving, in the morning pack *half* of the *chilled* beverage in a prechilled insulated vacuum bottle (see tip, page 46).

Bag Some Fresh Fruit

Fresh fruits make simply scrumptious additions to a brown-bag meal because you don't need to keep them chilled, and there are many that come in their own natural wrap for carrying. Choose your favorites from these good packables: apples, pears, oranges, red or green grapes, bananas, peaches, nectarines, apricots, plums, mangoes, dark sweet cherries, melon, papaya, or pineapple chunks. Pack cut-up fruits in airtight containers and don't forget a spoon. Extra napkins come in handy for juicy fruits, too.

English Toffee Cookies

1½ cups all-purpose flour
½ cup unsweetened cocoa powder
½ teaspoon baking soda

● In a medium bowl stir together the flour, cocoa powder, and baking soda. Set aside.

Watch out! These dark, chocolaty, chewy cookies don't change color very much as they bake; so be careful not to overbake them, or they'll be dry and hard. To test the cookies for doneness, gently touch them with your fingertip; the imprint should be barely visible.

½ cup butter or margarine
½ cup shortening
1 cup packed brown sugar
½ cup sugar
2 eggs
1 teaspoon vanilla
3 cups quick-cooking rolled oats
1 6-ounce package (1 cup) almond brickle pieces
1 6-ounce package (1 cup) semisweet chocolate pieces

● In a mixer bowl beat the butter or margarine and shortening with an electric mixer on medium speed for ½ minute. Add the brown sugar and sugar; beat till fluffy. Add eggs and vanilla; beat well.
  Add the flour mixture to the butter-sugar mixture. Beat on low speed just till well combined.
  Stir in the quick-cooking rolled oats, almond brickle pieces, and semisweet chocolate pieces.
  Drop dough by level tablespoonfuls 2 inches apart onto an ungreased cookie sheet. Bake in a 350° oven for 8 to 10 minutes or till done. Cool on wire rack.

● Pack 2 or 3 cookies together in small clear plastic bags or freezer bags. Store several days in a cool dry place or up to 4 months in the freezer. Makes about 48.

For a smaller batch, you can easily halve the recipe and make just two dozen cookies.

Apricot-Cashew Cookies

1 teaspoon finely shredded orange peel
¼ cup orange juice
⅓ cup snipped dried apricots

● In a small saucepan combine orange peel and orange juice. Bring to boiling. Add snipped apricots. Remove from heat and let stand 5 minutes. Drain the apricots, reserving the juice mixture.

Heating the apricots before mixing them into the cookie dough makes them plump and soft. Their tartness combines with orange juice and ginger to give these cakelike cookies extra-good flavor.

1½ cups all-purpose flour
½ teaspoon baking powder
½ teaspoon baking soda
¼ teaspoon ground ginger
½ cup butter or margarine
½ cup packed brown sugar
1 egg
1 teaspoon vanilla
½ cup chopped cashews

● Stir together flour, baking powder, soda, and ginger. Set aside. In a mixer bowl beat the butter or margarine with an electric mixer on medium speed for ½ minute. Add brown sugar and beat till fluffy. Add egg, reserved juice and peel, and vanilla; beat well. Add flour mixture; beat on low speed just till well combined. Stir in the apricots and cashews.
  Drop dough by rounded teaspoonfuls 2 inches apart onto a greased cookie sheet. Bake in a 375° oven for 10 minutes or till edges are golden. Cool cookies completely on a wire rack.

● Pack 2 or 3 cookies together in small clear plastic bags or freezer bags. Store several days in a cool dry place or up to 4 months in the freezer. Makes about 36.

Apple Cider-Bran Muffins

1½	cups whole bran cereal
1	cup apple cider *or* juice
1	beaten egg
¼	cup cooking oil
¼	cup maple-flavored syrup

● In a small bowl combine the bran cereal and apple cider or juice; let stand 3 minutes or till the liquid is absorbed. Stir in the egg, cooking oil, and maple-flavored syrup; set aside.

1	cup all-purpose flour
2	teaspoons baking powder
1	teaspoon ground cinnamon
¼	teaspoon baking soda
¼	teaspoon salt
1	medium apple, cored and finely chopped (1 cup)

● In a medium bowl stir together the flour, baking powder, ground cinnamon, baking soda, and salt. Make a well in the center. Add the bran-apple cider mixture all at once, stirring just till moistened. (Batter will be thick.) Fold in the chopped apple.

Grease muffin cups; fill ⅔ full. Bake in a 400° oven for 20 to 25 minutes. Remove from pans; cool.

● Pack 1 or 2 muffins together in small clear plastic bags or freezer bags. Store several days at room temperature or up to 4 months in the freezer. (Frozen muffins will thaw at room temperature in 4 to 6 hours.) Makes 10 to 12 muffins.

Take advantage of a microwave oven at work and try these muffins steaming hot, too. To reheat one or two muffins, put them on a *white* paper napkin or paper plate. Micro-cook, uncovered, on HIGH for 15 to 20 seconds.

Raisin Spice Cupcakes

1	cup all-purpose flour
⅓	cup sugar
½	teaspoon baking powder
½	teaspoon salt
½	teaspoon ground cinnamon
¼	teaspoon baking soda
¼	teaspoon ground cloves
¼	teaspoon ground nutmeg
⅓	cup packed brown sugar
⅓	cup shortening
½	cup buttermilk
1	egg
½	cup raisins
¼	cup chopped walnuts

● In a mixer bowl combine the flour, ⅓ cup sugar, baking powder, salt, the ½ teaspoon cinnamon, baking soda, cloves, and nutmeg.

Add the brown sugar, shortening, and buttermilk. Beat the mixture with an electric mixer on low speed just till the flour is moistened. Beat on medium speed for 2 minutes. Add egg. Beat 2 minutes more.

Stir in the raisins and chopped walnuts. Line muffin cups with paper bake cups. Fill ½ full.

4	teaspoons sugar
¼	teaspoon ground cinnamon

● Stir together the 4 teaspoons sugar and the ¼ teaspoon cinnamon. Sprinkle over batter, as shown at right. Bake in a 350° oven for 20 to 25 minutes. Cool completely on a wire rack.

We made these cupcakes brown-baggable by topping them with cinnamon-sugar instead of frosting. The sugar gives them sweet, crusty tops, and it won't make a mess in a brown bag the way frosting can.

● Pack each in a small clear plastic bag or freezer bag. Store several days at room temperature or up to 4 months in the freezer. (Frozen cupcakes will thaw at room temperature in 4 to 6 hours.) Makes 14 or 15 cupcakes.

Peanut Butter-Chip Muffins

1½ cups all-purpose flour
⅓ cup sugar
2½ teaspoons baking powder
¼ teaspoon salt
½ cup chunk-style
    peanut butter
2 tablespoons butter *or*
    margarine
2 beaten eggs
¾ cup milk
½ of a 6-ounce package
    (½ cup) semisweet
    chocolate pieces

● In a medium bowl stir together the flour, sugar, baking powder, and salt. With a pastry blender or 2 knives cut in the chunk-style peanut butter and the butter or margarine till the mixture resembles coarse crumbs.

In a small bowl combine the eggs and milk. Add all at once to the flour mixture. Stir just till moistened; batter should be lumpy. Fold in chocolate pieces. Grease muffin cups or line with paper bake cups. Fill ⅔ full, as shown below left. Bake in a 400° oven for 15 to 17 minutes or till lightly golden. Remove from muffin cups; cool on a wire rack.

Muffins make great additions to picnics, and satisfying snacking for camping trips or long car trips, too. Make a whole batch anytime, and freeze some for quick take-alongs later. (But be careful about muffin-snatchers, or you may not have enough left for brown-bag snacking!)

● Pack 1 or 2 together in small clear plastic bags or freezer bags, or pack several together in a freezer container. Store several days at room temperature or up to 4 months in the freezer. Makes 12 muffins.

After you've baked the muffins, remove them from the pans and cool. Then, pack the muffins together in an airtight container and store in the freezer up to four months. The muffins will thaw at room temperature in four to six hours.

Fill the greased or paper-bake-cup-lined muffin cups just two-thirds full. If you fill them full, the batter will run over as the muffins bake.

Apple-Cheddar Pastries

1 **package piecrust mix (for 2-crust pie)** ½ **cup dairy sour cream**	● For pastry, with a fork stir together the piecrust mix and sour cream till well blended. Form into ball; cover and chill.	**You can pack these eat-from-your-hand apple pies while they're still frozen. At room temperature, the pastries will thaw in four to six hours.**
½ **cup sugar** ½ **cup shredded sharp cheddar cheese (2 ounces)** 2 **teaspoons lemon juice** ½ **teaspoon ground cinnamon** 1 **pound cooking apples, peeled, cored, and chopped (about 3 cups)**	● In a large bowl stir together the ½ cup sugar, the shredded cheddar cheese, lemon juice, and ½ teaspoon ground cinnamon. Add the chopped apples. Toss to coat the apples with the sugar-cheese mixture.	
	● Divide the pastry into 12 pieces. On a floured surface roll each piece into a 5-inch circle. Place about *¼ cup* of the apple mixture just off-center on each pastry circle. Moisten edges of circle with a little water. Fold in half; seal by pressing with the tines of the fork.	
1 **tablespoon sugar** ½ **teaspoon ground cinnamon**	● Place on an ungreased baking sheet; prick tops. Combine the 1 tablespoon sugar and ½ teaspoon cinnamon; sprinkle over pastries. Bake in a 375° oven for 30 to 35 minutes or till crust is golden. Remove from baking sheet; cool completely on a wire rack.	
	● Pack each pastry in a small clear plastic bag or freezer bag. Store up to 1 week in the refrigerator or up to 1 month in the freezer. Makes 12 pastries.	

Sugar 'n' Spice Nuts

2½ **cups walnut halves** ¾ **cup sugar** 3 **tablespoons butter *or* margarine** ½ **teaspoon ground cinnamon** ½ **teaspoon finely shredded orange peel** ⅛ **teaspoon ground cloves** ⅛ **teaspoon salt**	● In a heavy 10-inch skillet combine the walnut halves, sugar, butter or margarine, ground cinnamon, finely shredded orange peel, ground cloves, and salt. Cook over medium heat, stirring constantly, for 7 to 9 minutes or till sugar is melted and nuts are toasted. Spread nuts on a buttered baking sheet or aluminum foil; separate into clusters. Cool completely.	**This candy-coated treat may leave your fingers a little sticky. For quick after-snacking cleanup, pack a dampened paper towel in a plastic bag.**
	● Pack ½-cup portions in small clear plastic bags. Store in a cool dry place. Makes 9 servings.	

Molasses-Popcorn Crunch

8 cups popped popcorn 1½ cups peanuts 1 cup coconut	● In a large roasting pan combine the popped popcorn, peanuts, and coconut.
¾ cup packed brown sugar 6 tablespoons butter *or* margarine 3 tablespoon molasses ⅛ teaspoon salt	● In a 1½-quart saucepan combine the brown sugar, butter or margarine, molasses, and salt. Cook and stir over medium heat till butter melts and mixture is boiling over entire surface. Cook for 5 minutes more over medium heat, stirring once or twice.
¼ teaspoon baking soda ¼ teaspoon vanilla	● Remove from heat. Stir in the baking soda and vanilla. Pour over popcorn mixture; stir gently to coat well, as shown at right. Bake in a 300° oven for 15 minutes; stir. Bake 5 minutes more. Remove baked popcorn mixture to a large bowl. Cool completely.
	● Pack 1-cup portions in small clear plastic bags. Store up to 1 week in a cool dry place. Makes 10 servings.

After you stir in the baking soda and vanilla, the syrup is still very hot. *Carefully* **pour it over the popcorn mixture; stir gently to coat all of the popcorn with the syrup.**

Hot-and-Spicy Party Mix

½ cup cooking oil 2 teaspoons paprika 1½ teaspoons chili powder ½ teaspoon onion powder ½ teaspoon salt ⅛ teaspoon bottled hot pepper sauce	● In a small saucepan combine the cooking oil, paprika, chili powder, onion powder, salt, and bottled hot pepper sauce. Cook and stir over low heat just till the mixture is warm.
5 cups bite-size corn squares cereal 2 cups round toasted oat cereal 1½ cups peanuts 1 cup small pretzels	● In a 13x9x2-inch baking pan combine the corn cereal, oat cereal, peanuts, and pretzels. Stir the oil and seasoning mixture well; drizzle over the cereal mixture, tossing to coat evenly. Bake in a 300° oven for 1 hour, stirring every 20 minutes. Cool completely.
	● Pack scant 1-cup portions in small clear plastic bags. Store in a cool dry place. Makes 10 servings.

How can you turn an ordinary snack break into a party? Pack several bags of this spicy, crisp mix to share. Then take along paper cups and an insulated vacuum bottle filled with your favorite cold beverage.

Molasses-Popcorn Crunch
(see recipe, page 61)

Fruit and Nut Mix

1 cup raisins
1 cup chopped mixed dried
   fruit
½ cup toasted whole
   almonds
½ cup coconut, toasted, *or*
   unsweetened coconut
   chips, toasted
½ cup dry roasted peanuts
½ of a 6-ounce package
   (½ cup) semisweet
   chocolate pieces
½ cup sunflower nuts

● In a medium bowl combine the
raisins, chopped mixed dried fruit,
toasted whole almonds, toasted coconut
or toasted unsweetened coconut chips,
dry roasted peanuts, semisweet chocolate
pieces, and sunflower nuts. Stir to mix all
the ingredients well.

● Pack ½-cup portions in small clear
plastic bags. Store in a cool dry place.
Makes 9 servings.

**When the weather is
warm, store this keep-
you-going trail mix in the
refrigerator so it stays
fresh and the chocolate
pieces stay firm.**

Sugar 'n' Spice Nuts
(see recipe, page 60)

Peanut Buttery Nibble Mix

3 cups corn-and-rice cereal
    bites *or* bite-size wheat,
    corn, or rice squares
    cereal
1 cup bite-size shredded
    wheat biscuits
1 cup salted peanuts
½ of a 6-ounce package
    (½ cup) peanut butter-
    flavored pieces
⅓ cup milk
⅓ cup semisweet chocolate
    pieces
⅓ cup raisins

● In a 13x9x2-inch baking pan combine the corn-and-rice cereal bites or bite-size squares cereal and the shredded wheat biscuits and salted peanuts. Stir to mix well. Set the mixture aside.

In a small saucepan combine the peanut butter-flavored pieces and milk. Cook and stir over low heat till the pieces are melted. Pour over the cereal mixture. Toss gently to coat well.

Bake in a 350° oven for 10 to 12 minutes or till the mixture is dry, stirring occasionally. Cool completely. Stir in the chocolate pieces and the raisins.

● Pack ½-cup portions in small clear plastic bags. Store in a cool dry place. Makes 10 servings.

Give your little brown baggers a surprise treat. Slip some of this sweet 'n' crunchy snack mix into their school lunches.

Early-Morning Turnovers

1 package (6) refrigerated biscuits
3 1-ounce slices Canadian-style bacon
1 5-ounce jar cheese spread with pineapple

● On a floured surface roll each biscuit into a 5-inch circle. Place one slice of Canadian-style bacon on each of *3* dough rounds. Top each slice with *2 rounded tablespoons* of cheese spread. Moisten the edges of the dough rounds with water. Top with remaining dough rounds. Press edges together with your fingers, making a fluted edge.

These breakfast sandwiches make hefty fare for camping meals, too. Add them, frozen, to your cooler in the evening just before you go. They'll be thawed and ready to eat by morning.

Milk
Sesame seed

● Brush the tops with milk; sprinkle with sesame seed. Place on an ungreased baking sheet. Bake in a 450° oven for 14 to 16 minutes or till golden brown. Cool on a wire rack up to 1 hour. Pack each turnover in a small clear plastic bag or freezer bag. Store up to 1 week in the refrigerator or up to 1 month in the freezer. Makes 3 servings.

● For *each* breakfast serving, in the morning pack *1 chilled* turnover in a brown bag. (Thaw frozen turnover overnight in the refrigerator.)

Breakfast Berry Soup

1 8-ounce can peach slices
½ cup plain yogurt
¼ cup orange juice
¼ cup nonfat dry milk powder
¼ teaspoon ground cinnamon

● In a blender container or food processor bowl combine the *undrained* peach slices, plain yogurt, orange juice, nonfat dry milk powder, and ground cinnamon. Cover and process till the mixture is smooth.

This fruit-filled soup makes a great lunchtime bag-stuffer, too. Take along one or two Apple Cider-Bran Muffins (see recipe, page 57) for a satisfying meal anytime.

¼ cup chopped walnuts
¼ cup fresh *or* frozen blueberries, raspberries, *or* sliced strawberries, thawed

● Stir in chopped walnuts and berries. Cover and store up to 2 days in the refrigerator. Makes 2 (1-cup) servings.

● For *each* breakfast serving, in the morning pour *half* of the *chilled* berry soup into a prechilled insulated vacuum bottle (see tip, page 46).

Peanut Butter Granola

3 cups rolled oats 1 cup coconut 1 cup unsalted peanuts ½ cup sunflower nuts ½ cup toasted wheat germ	● In a bowl stir together the rolled oats, coconut, unsalted peanuts, sunflower nuts, and toasted wheat germ. Set aside.
⅔ cup peanut butter ½ cup light corn syrup ¼ cup packed brown sugar 2 tablespoons cooking oil	● In a small saucepan combine the peanut butter, corn syrup, brown sugar, and cooking oil. Cook and stir over medium heat till the peanut butter is melted and the brown sugar is dissolved. Pour the peanut butter mixture over the oat mixture. Stir till combined.
½ cup chopped pitted dates ½ cup raisins	● Spread mixture in a 15x10x1-inch baking pan. Bake in a 300° oven for 45 to 50 minutes, stirring every 15 minutes. Stir in the dates and raisins. Cool the granola completely.
	● Pack ¼- to ½-cup portions in small clear plastic bags. Store in a cool dry place or in the refrigerator. Makes about 8 cups granola.

How many ways can you eat granola for breakfast? You can eat it with milk, just like other cereals. (Don't forget to carry the milk in an insulated vacuum bottle, and take a plastic spoon, too.) Or, stir the granola into your favorite flavor of yogurt. But for easiest eating, try munching this full-of-peanuts granola straight, right from the bag.

Date-Nut Breakfast Bagels

1 3-ounce package cream cheese, softened 1 tablespoon orange juice 2 tablespoons snipped pitted whole dates 2 tablespoons chopped pecans	● In a small bowl stir together the softened cream cheese and orange juice till smooth. Stir in the snipped dates and chopped pecans.
2 whole wheat *or* egg bagels, split	● Spread *half* of the cream cheese mixture onto the bottom half of *each* bagel. Top with remaining half. Pack each sandwich in a small clear plastic bag or freezer bag. Store up to 1 week in the refrigerator or up to 1 month in the freezer. Makes 2 servings.
	● For *each* breakfast serving, carry *1 chilled* sandwich in a brown bag. (Thaw frozen sandwich overnight in the refrigerator before packing.)

With these bagelwiches, we've turned a breakfast favorite into an easy-to-carry morning meal. They're stuffed with tangy cream cheese, sweet dried fruit, and crunchy nuts.

Crunchy Bacon Muffins

½ pound bacon (10 to 12
    slices)

1¾ cups all-purpose flour
¼ cup sugar
1 tablespoon baking powder

    Cooking oil
1 beaten egg
¾ cup milk

1 cup shredded chedda
    cheese (4 ounces)
½ cup Grape Nuts cere

● I ...ll crisp; drain,
res... ; set
cr...

gol...
completel...

Take a can of cold fruit
juice to sip with these
muffins. Wrap it in a
...ll plastic bag before
...That way,
...rom the chilled
...soak your food
...rown bag.

● Pack 1 or 2 muffins tog...
clear plastic bags or freezer bags.
up to 1 week in the refrigerator or up to
4 months in the freezer. (Thaw frozen
muffins overnight in the refrigerator
before packing.) Makes 12 muffins.

Brown-Bagger Breakfasts

The tasty recipes on these two pages make great
breakfasts on the run. Give each the protein boost that
will make it a complete meal by including a hard-
cooked egg, yogurt, cheese, milk, or nuts in your
brown bag. And remember, if you won't be eating
your breakfast within one or two hours of packing it,
you'll need to keep the cold foods cold by carrying
them in an insulated lunch box with a frozen ice pack.

Picnic Pointers

For a picnic that'll come off without a hitch, remember these take-along tips. (1) Make it simple: Choose foods that are easy to prepare, serve, and eat. (2) Be organized: Write a list of everything you'll need. Make all the foods ahead and pack them for convenient serving. (3) Keep it safe: To prevent spoilage, serve hot foods hot and cold foods cold. Here are a few more meal-toting hints that will ensure safe, enjoyable, and hassle-free picnics.

- Cut fresh vegetables and fruits into easy-to-eat pieces. Take along a favorite savory dip for the vegetables, and a sweet dip for the fruit pieces.

- For easy main dishes, choose already-cooked ham, roast beef, or poultry. Slice the meat or poultry before you go.

- Add muffins or rolls to your cooler or picnic basket. Pack butter, margarine, or other spreads in small airtight containers; carry in the cooler.

- Food can spoil quickly outdoors, especially in the hot sun. To keep food safe, be sure everything that touches picnic food, including your hands, is very clean.

- Keep cold foods covered and in the refrigerator until you leave. Then, pack them in an insulated container with a frozen ice pack.

- When you take a hot food, pack that just before you leave, too. Use an insulated container, such as a plastic-foam covered casserole, and pack the food as soon as it comes out of the oven or off the range.

- Make sure foods that require no heating or chilling are well wrapped. Then pack them separately in a picnic basket, box, or large paper bag.

- At the picnic site, don't leave meats, poultry, fish, or dairy products out after serving. Return leftovers to the cooler or insulated lunch box.

- Avoid taking custards, puddings, and other egg-thickened dishes. They can break down and spoil.

- Carry hot and cold beverages—such as coffee, tea, lemonade, and fruit juice—in large insulated vacuum bottles. To keep drinks hot or cold longer, preheat or prechill insulated vacuum bottles before filling (see tip, page 46).

- Don't forget to pack a tablecloth or blanket, paper plates or bowls, plastic eating and serving utensils, plenty of paper napkins, salt and pepper shakers, cups for your beverage, and paper towels for spills and cleanup. (To take care of sticky fingers, dampen some of the paper towels and wrap them in small plastic bags before you leave home.)

Anytime Picnic for Two

Whether it's to celebrate the first warm spring day, to wind up a summer bike ride, to revel in fall colors, or to enjoy an indoors-by-the-fire evening in winter, a picnic is a delightful way to share a meal. So put together our elegant totable menu for two. Follow the countdown on the opposite page and you're guaranteed easy preparation, great food, and fun!

MENU

Roast Beef Salad
Poppy Seed Bread Twists
Cranberry and
   Dried Fruit Compote
   (see pages 72 and 73)
Red Burgundy or Rosé wine

MENU COUNTDOWN

Night before:

Prepare the beef mixture for *Roast Beef Salad;* pack and chill. Prepare *Cranberry and Dried Fruit Compote;* pack and chill. Prepare *Poppy Seed Twists;* cool and wrap in a plastic bag.

Just before you go:

Pack salad greens and tomatoes in plastic bags. Place the *chilled* beef mixture, *chilled* compote, greens, and tomatoes into an insulated lunch box or cooler. Fill a picnic basket with a blanket, plates, forks, knives, spoons, dessert glasses, napkins, bread twists, a bottle of wine, a corkscrew, and wineglasses.

At serving time:

Divide the salad greens, tomatoes, and beef mixture between two plates. Serve the compote in dessert glasses.

Roast Beef Salad

¼ cup mayonnaise *or* salad dressing
3 tablespoons milk
2 tablespoons dairy sour cream
2 tablespoons grated Parmesan cheese
¼ teaspoon dried oregano, crushed
Dash garlic powder

● For dressing, in a small bowl combine the mayonnaise or salad dressing, milk, sour cream, grated Parmesan cheese, crushed oregano, and garlic powder. Stir till well mixed.

4 ounces cooked roast beef, cut into thin bite-size strips (¾ cup)
¼ cup very thinly sliced carrots
¼ cup chopped green pepper

● In a medium bowl toss together the roast beef strips, sliced carrots, and chopped green pepper. Add the dressing; toss to coat. Pack in an airtight container. Store several hours or overnight in the refrigerator. (If necessary, stir in a little more milk after chilling.) Makes 2 servings.

3 cups torn salad greens
½ cup halved cherry tomatoes
⅓ cup croutons (optional)

● For 2 servings, just before leaving pack the salad greens and halved cherry tomatoes in separate clear plastic bags. Carry the *chilled* beef mixture, the salad greens, and the tomatoes in an insulated lunch box with a frozen ice pack. If desired, pack the croutons in a plastic bag and add to the lunch box.
    At serving time, divide the salad greens and tomatoes between 2 serving plates or bowls. Spoon beef mixture atop. Sprinkle with croutons, if desired.

The beef and the Parmesan cheese will soak up some of the liquid from the dressing as the mixture chills. The longer it chills, the thicker the dressing will be. Check the beef mixture just before packing for your picnic. If it's thick rather than creamy, stir in 1 to 2 tablespoons of milk.

Cranberry and Dried Fruit Compote

1 cup mixed dried fruits
1½ cups cranberry juice
    cocktail
1 tablespoon brown sugar
¼ teaspoon ground
    cinnamon
2 tablespoons brandy
	● Cut up large pieces of the dried fruit. In a small saucepan combine the fruit, cranberry juice cocktail, brown sugar, and cinnamon. Bring mixture to boiling; reduce heat. Cover and simmer for 10 minutes or till the fruit is tender. Stir in the brandy. Pack in an airtight container. Store several hours or overnight in the refrigerator. Makes 2 servings.	**Serve this saucy compote in dessert glasses or wineglasses. (For safe carrying, wrap the glasses in cloth napkins before packing.) Then, when you've eaten the fruit, sip the deliciously sweet and spicy liquid as an after-dinner drink.**

	● For 2 servings, just before leaving pack the container of *chilled* compote with Roast Beef Salad in an insulated lunch box with a frozen ice pack.	

Poppy Seed Twists

1 package (6) refrigerated biscuits	● Cut each biscuit in half. With your hands, roll each biscuit half into an 8-inch rope, moistening hands, if necessary. (Ropes will shrink to about 6 inches.)	**Take along a pretty little basket and a cloth napkin to your picnic. At mealtime, line the basket with the napkin and arrange these little bread sticks in it.**
Milk Poppy seed *or* sesame seed	● Tightly twist two of the ropes together. Place on a greased baking sheet at least 3 inches apart. Repeat to make 6 twists. Brush tops of the twists with milk. Sprinkle poppy seed or sesame seed over each twist. Bake in a 450° oven for 6 minutes. Cool completely on a wire rack.	
	● Pack cooled twists together in a clear plastic bag. Store in a cool dry place till packing for picnic. Carry in a picnic basket or in the insulated lunch box. Makes 6 twists.	

Crispy Orange Chicken

30 shredded wheat wafers, broken (2½ cups) ¼ cup sunflower nuts ⅛ teaspoon garlic powder	● In a blender container or food processor bowl combine the shredded wheat wafers, sunflower nuts, and garlic powder. Cover and process till finely crushed. Spread the crumb mixture on a sheet of waxed paper.
1 beaten egg ½ teaspoon finely shredded orange peel ⅓ cup fresh orange juice (1 orange)	● In a bowl combine the beaten egg, finely shredded orange peel, and orange juice; stir to mix well.
1 2½- to 3-pound broiler-fryer chicken, cut up	● Rinse chicken pieces; pat dry with paper towels. Dip each chicken piece in the egg-orange juice mixture. Roll in the crumb mixture to coat. Arrange the chicken, skin side up, in a 15½x10½x2-inch baking pan, making sure pieces don't touch. Bake, uncovered, in a 375° oven about 50 minutes or till the chicken is tender. *Do not turn.*
	● Cool the chicken on paper towels on a wire rack for 30 minutes; cover loosely and chill in the refrigerator. When the chicken is thoroughly chilled, pack in an airtight container. Store overnight in the refrigerator. Makes 4 to 6 servings.
	● For 4 servings, just before leaving pack the container of *chilled* chicken in a cooler with a frozen ice pack.

AN EASY OLD-FASHIONED PICNIC
This make-ahead menu boasts old-fashioned goodness with newfangled ease. Follow our countdown and you're guaranteed an enjoyable picnic from start to finish.
MENU
Crispy Orange Chicken
Minted Fruit Toss
Molasses-Date Bars
Lemonade, coffee, or tea
Night before:
Prepare *Crispy Orange Chicken;* chill, pack, and store as directed. Prepare *Minted Fruit Toss;* pack and chill.
Night before or early the same day:
Prepare *Molasses-Date Bars.* Cool completely. Pack in an airtight container.
Just before you go:
Pack a cooler with a frozen ice pack. Add chilled *Crispy Orange Chicken* and *Minted Fruit Toss.* Pack a picnic basket with a blanket or tablecloth, salt and pepper shakers, paper plates and napkins, and plastic spoons, forks, cups. Add bars and an insulated vacuum bottle filled with lemonade, coffee, or tea.
Note: Keep chilled foods in cooler till serving time.

Minted Fruit Toss

2 tablespoons mayonnaise *or* salad dressing 2 tablespoons lemon yogurt 2 teaspoons snipped fresh mint *or* ½ teaspoon dried mint, crushed	● In a small bowl stir together the mayonnaise or salad dressing, lemon yogurt, and snipped or crushed mint.	**This refreshing fruit salad makes a delicious addition to everyday brown-bag lunches, too. For *one* serving, pack ¾ cup of the salad in a small airtight container. Store up to one week in the refrigerator. Carry chilled salad in an insulated lunch box with a frozen ice pack.**
2 cups cubed cantaloupe 1 cup halved fresh strawberries 1 8-ounce can pineapple chunks, drained	● Combine the cantaloupe, strawberries, and pineapple. Add the mayonnaise-yogurt mixture; toss to coat. Pack in an airtight container. Store the fruit mixture several hours or overnight in the refrigerator. Makes 4 servings.	
	● For 4 servings, just before leaving pack the container of *chilled* fruit mixture with Crispy Orange Chicken in a cooler with a frozen ice pack.	

Molasses-Date Bars

2 eggs ¾ cup sugar 1 teaspoon vanilla ½ cup molasses	● In a bowl beat together the eggs, sugar, and vanilla. Add the molasses to the egg mixture; stir to mix well.	**For easy serving, pack these moist, chocolaty bars between layers of waxed paper to keep them from sticking together.**
½ cup butter *or* margarine 2 squares (2 ounces) unsweetened chocolate	● In a large saucepan melt the butter or margarine and chocolate; remove from heat. Stir in the egg mixture.	
¾ cup all-purpose flour ½ cup quick-cooking rolled oats ½ teaspoon baking powder ¼ teaspoon baking soda ¼ teaspoon salt ½ cup chopped dates	● In a bowl stir together the flour, quick-cooking rolled oats, baking powder, baking soda, and salt. Stir the flour mixture into the chocolate mixture. Stir in the chopped dates.	
Sifted powdered sugar	● Spread the batter in a greased 9x9x2-inch baking pan. Bake in a 350° oven for 25 to 30 minutes. Cool completely on a wire rack; dust the top with the powdered sugar. Cut into bars.	
	● Pack cooled bars in an airtight container. Carry in a picnic basket. Makes 24 bars.	

Kids' 1-2-3 Lunch

Making your own lunch is as easy as 1-2-3 with just a little help from a grown-up.

MENU
Peanut Butter Granwich
Filled-with-Fruit Yogurt
Fruit Juice

Night before:
1. Put an ice pack into the freezer. Put a small can of fruit juice into the refrigerator.
2. Make the *Filled-with-Fruit Yogurt.* Chill in the refrigerator.
3. Make the *Peanut Butter Granwich.* Pack and chill.

Early in the morning:
Put the *frozen* ice pack, *Filled-with-Fruit Yogurt, Peanut Butter Granwich,* and juice into an insulated lunch box.

Filled-with-Fruit Yogurt

EQUIPMENT

table knife	measuring spoon
sharp knife	rubber scraper
cutting board	airtight container
measuring cups	ice pack
small bowl	insulated lunch box

Make this yummy fruit salad first, because you'll want to have a grown-up help you cut the fruit. Then, you can go on and make the sandwich by yourself.

Next time, be different and try the salad with orange, raspberry, or peach yogurt.

1 orange
¼ cup strawberries *or* seedless grapes

● Use a table knife to make a cut in the orange peel. Use your fingers to take the peel off the orange. Ask an adult to help you use a sharp knife and a cutting board to cut the orange into slices. Cut each slice in half crosswise. Cut the strawberries or grapes in half. Put the orange pieces and the strawberry or grape halves into a small bowl.

2 tablespoons chopped pecans *or* coconut (optional)
⅓ cup strawberry yogurt

● If you like, put the chopped pecans or the coconut into the bowl. Use a rubber scraper to push the yogurt out of the measuring cup into the bowl. Stir to mix well. Spoon the mixture into an airtight container. Store overnight in the refrigerator. Makes 1 serving.

● For 1 serving, in the morning pack the container of the *chilled* yogurt and fruit mixture in an insulated lunch box with a frozen ice pack.

Peanut Butter Granwich

EQUIPMENT

measuring spoons	insulated lunch box
table knife	and ice pack, *or*
plastic bag	brown bag

If you'd like to eat the Peanut Butter Granwich for lunch *without* the Filled-with-Fruit Yogurt, you can carry the sandwich in a brown bag without an ice pack.

2 slices whole wheat bread
2 tablespoons peanut butter
1 tablespoon grape jelly
2 tablespoons granola
1 tablespoon raisins

● Use a table knife to spread *1 slice* of bread with the peanut butter and the jelly. Sprinkle the granola over the jelly. Sprinkle with the raisins. Put the *second slice* of bread on top. Use the table knife to cut the sandwich in half. Pack the sandwich in a small clear plastic bag. Store it overnight in the refrigerator. Makes 1 sandwich.

● For 1 serving, in the morning pack the sandwich in an insulated lunch box with a frozen ice pack or in a brown bag (see tip at right).

Hot Dog Soup

EQUIPMENT

can opener	measuring cup
rubber scraper	measuring spoon
saucepan	wooden spoon
table knife	airtight containers
ruler	vacuum bottle

1 10¾-ounce can condensed tomato soup
2 or 3 plain hot dogs *or* hot dogs with cheese (5 ounces)
¾ cup milk
½ teaspoon Worcestershire sauce

● Scrape soup into a saucepan. Cut hot dogs into ½-inch slices. Add to saucepan. Add milk and Worcestershire sauce. Ask an adult to help you cook and stir on medium heat till bubbly. Divide between 2 airtight containers or freezer containers. Store up to 1 week in the refrigerator or up to 1 month in the freezer. Makes 2 (1½-cup) servings.

● For *each* serving, in the morning ask an adult to help you reheat the soup from *1 container* before packing it in a preheated insulated vacuum bottle (see tip, page 46).

Super Cookies

EQUIPMENT

measuring cups	cutting board
measuring spoons	meat mallet
medium bowl	cookie sheet
wooden spoon	ruler
table knife	hot pads
electric mixer	pancake turner
plastic bags	cooling rack

2 cups all-purpose flour
2 teaspoons baking powder
1 teaspoon baking soda
¾ cup peanut butter
¼ cup butter *or* margarine
1½ cups packed brown sugar
2 eggs
¼ cup molasses
1 teaspoon vanilla
1 cup quick-cooking rolled oats
1 cup coarsely crushed salted peanuts (see tip at far right)
1 cup raisins

● Put the flour, baking powder, and soda into a medium bowl. Use a wooden spoon to stir till well mixed.

Ask an adult to help you beat peanut butter and butter with an electric mixer on medium speed for ½ minute. Add brown sugar. Beat till fluffy. Add eggs, molasses, and vanilla. Beat till well mixed. Add flour mixture. Stir till mixed. Stir in oats, peanuts, and raisins.

For *each* cookie, spoon ⅓ cup dough onto an ungreased cookie sheet. Flatten into a 3½-inch circle. Leave 2 inches between circles. Bake in a 350° oven for 12 to 14 minutes. Cool 1 minute, then move to a cooling rack. Cool completely.

● Pack *each* cookie in a small clear plastic bag or freezer bag. Store several days in a cool dry place or up to 1 month in the freezer. Makes 15 cookies.

A SCHOOL-DAY HOT LUNCH FOR KIDS
Make your school lunch the envy of all the other kids with these tasty recipes. The Super Cookies are great fun to make on a long, rainy afternoon.
MENU
Hot Dog Soup
Super Cookie
Apple or Dried Fruit
Milk
Up to a week ahead:
Make *Super Cookies.* Cool completely. Pack each cookie in a small plastic bag. Store in a cool dry place.
Night before:
Make *Hot Dog Soup.* Pack in airtight containers. Store in the refrigerator overnight.
Early the same day:
Reheat the soup; ask an adult to help you pour it into an insulated vacuum bottle. Cover tightly with the lid. Pour cold milk into another insulated vacuum bottle. (Or, if you can buy milk at lunchtime, take along some change.) Put an apple or some dried fruit into a small clear plastic bag. Pack everything together in a clean brown bag or lunch box.

To chop the peanuts, put them into one plastic bag inside a second plastic bag. Close the bags. On a cutting board, use the flat side of a meat mallet to lightly pound the nuts till they are coarsely crushed.

Index

Quick Packing:

For easy brown bagging, try these recipes you can make ahead and pack straight from the freezer.

Tips: